WISDOM
from Above

volume two

WISDOM
from Above

volume two

DR. BETTY R. PRICE

FAITH ONE
PUBLISHING

WISDOM FROM ABOVE, Vol. 2 by Dr. Betty R. Price
Published by Faith One Publishing
7901 S. Vermont Avenue
Los Angeles, CA 90044

This book is produced and distributed by Creation House, a part of Strang Communications, www.creationhouse.com.

Unless otherwise noted, all Scripture quotations are from the New King James Version of the Bible. Copyright © 1979, 1980, 1982 by Thomas Nelson, Inc., publishers. Used by permission.

Scripture quotations marked KJV are from the King James Version of the Bible.

Unless otherwise noted, all definitions are from the *Spirit-Filled Life Bible*. Copyright © 1991 by Thomas Nelson, Inc., publishers.

Design Director: Bill Johnson
Cover design by Justin Evans

Library of Congress Control Number: 2007931870
International Standard Book Number: 978-1-59979-382-5

First Edition

08 09 10 11 12 — 9 8 7 6 5 4 3 2 1
Printed in the United States of America

CONTENTS

INTRODUCTION

Almost every day I hear about another Christian who has allowed Satan to ensnare him or her. We live in perilous times, and there is just too much to accomplish before our Savior can return for the church. In Proverbs, the book of wisdom, we read that wisdom is the ability to live life skillfully by successfully applying the Word of God to our lives. Proverbs 2:1–12 tells it like this:

> My son, if you receive my words, And treasure my commands within you, So that you incline your ear to wisdom, And apply your heart to understanding; Yes, if you cry out for discernment, And lift up your voice for understanding, If you seek her as silver, And search for her as for hidden treasures; Then you will understand the fear of the Lord, And find the knowledge of God. For the Lord gives wisdom; From His mouth come knowledge and understanding; He stores up sound wisdom for the upright; He is a shield to those who walk uprightly; He guards the paths of justice, And preserves the way of His saints. Then you will understand righteousness and justice, Equity and every good path. When wisdom enters your heart,

And knowledge is pleasant to your soul, Discretion will preserve you; Understanding will keep you, To deliver you from the way of evil.

In the second volume of *Wisdom From Above*, I plan to further discuss how to grow in God's wisdom and understand just how important His wisdom is to our lives. If we want to be used by God and to complete our divine assignment we must be vigilant about how we conduct our lives and what we are dwelling on behind closed doors and in those private moments. Always remember that Satan can only be involved in your life to the extent you allow him. He has no power or authority over the Christian. However, to keep him under your feet you must "submit to God. Resist the devil and he will flee from you" (James 4:7).

I encourage you to know that the Bible is not just to be read and put on your nightstand. It is life to all who discover its truths. Seek life. If you do, you will live abundantly and blessed, just as God has promised.

—DR. BETTY R. PRICE

CHAPTER I

THE HIGH CALLING OF GOD

I press toward the mark for the prize...the high calling of God.

—PHILIPPIANS 3:14, KJV

WHAT IS THE HIGH CALLING of God? Sadly, many Christians today still do not know what we are called to be or what we are called to do. In other words, we do not know what our real purpose is in this life.

Galatians 3:26 says:

> For you are all sons of God through faith in Christ Jesus.

We are called to be sons and daughters in Jesus Christ, or stated another way, we are called to *sonship* in Christ. Likewise, John 1:12 tells us:

> But as many as received Him, to them He gave the right to become children of God, to those who believe in His name.

We are called to be God's children, His family in the earth realm. Whether you know it or not, it is a wonderful privilege to be called to the family of God. Because we have this wonderful call to sonship with God, the apostle John tells us we should purify ourselves to be like Jesus:

> Behold what manner of love the Father has bestowed on us, that we should be called children of God! Therefore, the world does not know us, because it did not know Him. Beloved, now we are children of God; and it has not yet been revealed what we shall be, but we know that when He is revealed, we shall be like Him, for we shall see Him as He is. And everyone who has this hope in Him purifies himself, just as He is pure.
>
> —1 JOHN 3:1–3

The word *pure* is an adjective which describes a person or thing as "being clean, modest, pure, undefiled, morally faultless, and without blemish." Our total lifestyle should be lived as a praise to God. Whatever we do, if God cannot get the glory out of it, we should not be doing it. If we learn that and make rules for ourselves, we can go through this life enjoying the benefits and blessings that Jesus provided for us. First Peter 2:9 says:

> But you are a chosen generation, a royal priesthood, a holy nation, His own special people, that you may proclaim the praises of Him who called you out of darkness into His marvelous light.

Ephesians 4:1–6 tells us more about the walk and the calling as God's children.

> I, therefore, the prisoner of the Lord, beseech you to walk worthy of the calling with which you were called, with all lowliness and gentleness...
>
> —Ephesians 4:1–2

Lowliness means "modesty, humility, a sense of moral insignificance, and a humble attitude of unselfish concern for the welfare of others." If we all lived that way, no one in the body of Christ would go lacking in anything. The word *gentleness* describes a disposition that is balanced in spirit, unpretentious, and self-controlled. The word is best translated as *meekness*. It is not an indication of weakness but of power and strength under control. A lot of people mistake kindness for weakness. A person who has this quality pardons injuries, corrects faults, and rules his spirit well.

> ...with longsuffering, bearing with one another in love, endeavoring to keep the unity of the Spirit in the bond of peace. There is one body and one Spirit, just as you were called in one hope of your calling; one Lord, one faith, one baptism; one God and Father of all, who is above all, and through all, and in you all.
>
> —Ephesians 4:2–6

Longsuffering means "patience, endurance, which is the ability to stand, persevering, tolerating, putting up with, standing firm, and not losing courage under pressure."

We are family, and we should want to look out for one another, as God looks out for us. How do we walk in that calling? You walk in that calling by putting on the *new man.* Ephesians 4:24 says:

> And that you put on the new man which was created according to God, in true righteousness and holiness.

The point I want to stress here is that it is up to us to put on the new man. Even though God has called us to be His children, He is not going to put on the new man for us. We do that. We have to put on holiness. We have to be determined to live the holy life.

Now notice where Ephesians 4:24 says, "The new man which was created...in *true* righteousness and holiness" (emphasis added). That means there could be a false righteousness or false holiness. Some denominations and churches have taught a lot of false holiness, which has nothing to do with real holiness. Some of these ideas prohibit makeup or certain kinds of clothes, jewelry, and things like that. These acts are not signs of true holiness, and too many times these practices can lead to false holiness, because some people who do all these things are not living holy. God says, "Put on...true holiness." There are too many Christians who claim that they are holy because of what they wear and where they go or don't go, but they are not living according to the Word.

Some of us have been Christians long enough that we should be walking in a higher calling than we are. We should be at a point where we can help others by our example. A lot of us can't help others because we have never matured spiritually ourselves. Ephesians 5:1 instructs us to "be imitators of God as dear children." Maybe some of us still don't know who God is and what He does, so we don't know how to imitate Him. We know He is a holy God, and we know He is a righteous God. We know He is a "does-right" God. However, you can't imitate Him if that's all you know about His character. The only way you are going to know Him is by spending time getting into the Word and praying in the Spirit (that is, praying with tongues), so you can strengthen your spirit man.

When we become imitators of God, we will not deliberately say or do things to hurt people. Sometimes people just hurt others without even thinking about what they are saying, and the way to avoid this is to be more like God, because we know God is love.

> And walk in love, as Christ also has loved us and given Himself for us, an offering and a sacrifice to God for a sweet-smelling aroma.
> —EPHESIANS 5:2

When we think about all that Jesus has done for us, we should be so grateful to Him that we would want to imitate Him.

Fornication

I talk against fornication just about every time I minister because it is still so prevalent among the body of Christ. Every year at our church we find out someone in helps ministry (the group of church volunteers that assist us in the day-to-day operation of this ministry) is having a problem with fornication, and we have to ask them to sit down from their position until they can get their act together. It is a shame, because we talk against it over and over, and yet people still do it. They have to know it is wrong, but they cannot seem to discipline their bodies. Evidently, it was also common when Paul was ministering, because he talked about it in almost all of his epistles.

> But fornication and all uncleanness or covetousness, let it not even be named among you, as is fitting for saints.
>
> —EPHESIANS 5:3

> Now concerning the things of which you wrote to me: It is good for a man not to touch a woman. ["To touch" is talking about having sex with someone you are not married to.]
>
> —1 CORINTHIANS 7:1

The *Spirit-Filled Life Bible* notes, "It has been argued that as the stomach is designed for food, the genitals are created for sexual experience. As when one is hungry, one eats. So when one is sexually aroused, one gratifies sexual passions. Not so. You can't put those two into the same category."[1] Because of the God-ordained purposes of the body, the digestive and sexual functions of the body are not in the same category. Some people think that they are. They think that because they get hungry, they should eat. And because they feel like they need sex, they should have sex. But it is not so.

I want to quote something else I read from the *Spirit-Filled Life Bible* that I think fits right here:

> Eating food is a secondary and temporary arrangement. But sexuality reaches into the depths of one's being. It goes further than the body. Because of God's resurrection design for the body, an essential identity exists between the present physical body and the future glorified body.
>
> Sexual intercourse is more than a biological experience. It involves a communion of life. Since Jesus is one with the believer's spirit, you are causing Him to be involved in immorality [if you get involved in sex outside of marriage]. Sexuality is a uniquely profound aspect of the personality, involving one's whole being. Sexual immorality has far-reaching effects and great spiritual significance and social complications. [That is so true; I have counseled many people who have been messed up because of their sexuality.]
>
> Such immorality is not a sin against the body; it is a sin against the Holy Spirit, who dwells in the body. Because believers have been purchased by the blood of Christ, they should honor Him to whom they belong, because He paid the highest price that could be paid. We should think about that and honor Him. He would not tell you to do something that you could not do.[2]

So then, what do we do about our sexuality? When we feel like we need sex, what do we do with that desire? We do what Romans 12:1–2 says to do:

> I beseech you therefore, brethren, by the mercies
> of God, that you present your bodies a living
> sacrifice, holy, acceptable to God, which is your
> reasonable service. And do not be conformed to
> this world, but be transformed by the renewing of
> your mind, that you may prove what is that good
> and acceptable and perfect will of God.

When temptation comes to have sex outside of marriage and your body is telling you that you cannot live without sex, you do what Paul tells you: present your bodies a living sacrifice, deny yourself, and commit your life to the Lord. He will help you overcome. When those urges come, you tell your body, "You belong to the Lord." If you do that, you won't get into trouble. It is just that simple, and when you do this you can have peace of mind.

The world does all kind of ungodly things and keeps what it is doing before our eyes, like everything is all right. This is what happened in Sodom and Gomorrah. The people got so involved in sexual sin that it became common and acceptable. It is the same way in the world today. People live together as if they are married and think nothing of it, including some who profess to be Christians. If you get involved in illicit sex with one of these no-good men or women telling you what they are going to give you if you give in, you may end up with a venereal disease, AIDS, a child out of wedlock, and low self-esteem.

I got a call from a lady who was messed up because of her sexuality. Her self-esteem was in the toilet. She had been married to a minister, but he had died and another minister tried to get involved with her. (That goes to show you that no matter how saved you are, the body is not changed. If you do certain things to turn it on, it is going to get you into trouble.) She was the last one living in her family, so she had no one to go to talk to when her husband died. When that other minister came along, she was just looking for someone to love her. She ended up having an affair with him. Then, because he was a minister, the guilt did her up badly. After the affair ended, he told her he didn't want to marry her; he said she was just a "quickie." She felt so terrible by the time he left her that she just had to see someone. She came to me for help, and I gave her the Word. She realized that though she had been looking for love, all she had with the minister was lust, because he ended up leaving her. As a result, she was in much worse shape than she was in before she began the affair with him. That is why God tells us not to get into these sexual affairs; nine times out of ten, you will end up getting hurt.

I worked with this lady for a couple of years when I introduced her to a Christian man I knew whose wife had died ten years ago. He was just the sweetest person in the world, and he had not remarried. It had to be God. This guy started talking to her when she was low in spirit and still messed up, but he and I just kept building her up. With this wonderful, kind man working with her, they ended up falling in love. Not too long after, they got married.

Keep in mind that when you think God doesn't know what is going on with you, He knows. That is why He tells us not to get into sin, because it will tear our self-esteem down. It isn't just about fornication or even getting pregnant out of wedlock; there are a lot of other things Christians do that are a lot worse. There is a lot of stuff on the inside of us that we need to get rid of. You can't go by how you feel or what your body is telling you. Go by what God says in His Word.

Guard Your Mind and Your Mouth

> Neither filthiness, nor foolish talking, nor coarse jesting, which are not fitting, but rather giving of thanks.
>
> —EPHESIANS 5:4

In Ephesians 4:29 the Scriptures warn us to only speak those things that edify. Otherwise, don't say anything. We always have to be aware that wherever we are we represent Christ. Besides that, speaking and dwelling on worldly things keeps your mind thinking about things that can lead to sin.

> For you were once darkness, but now you are light in the Lord. Walk as children of light [or, "children of God"] (for the fruit of the Spirit is in all goodness, righteousness, and truth), finding out what is acceptable to the Lord. And have no fellowship with the unfruitful works of darkness, but rather expose them. For it is shameful even to speak of those things which are done by them in secret.
>
> —EPHESIANS 5:8–12

We shouldn't be telling things that we would not want the Lord to hear in our conversations.

But all things that are exposed are made manifest by the light, for whatever makes manifest is light. Therefore He says: "Awake, you who sleep, Arise from the dead, And Christ will give you light. See then that you walk circumspectly, not as fools but as wise, redeeming the time, because the days are evil. Therefore do not be unwise, but understand what the will of the Lord is.

—EPHESIANS 5:13–16

It is our responsibility to understand what the will of the Lord is, because it is revealed to us in His Word.

The believer's day-to-day walk is crucial to the cause of Christ and to the welfare of society. We either contribute to the building up or the tearing down of society. We carry the message of life or death by our Christian walk. If wise, we present life. If unwise, we present death. Therefore, we don't want to walk in death ourselves or present death to anyone else.

We need to walk carefully and strictly by redeeming the time. Just think how much time we waste when we are involved in something that we have no business being involved in. Don't waste your time thinking or moping around about what you can't do, how much money you don't have, or where you can't go. What does all of this have to do with anything? Just do what you can to prosper the kingdom of God. Work with what you have. The rewards are well worth it in the end. We could do a lot of things for the kingdom if we would just get out of ourselves and get into Jesus Christ.

Dwell on the Word, Not Your Circumstances

I counsel with single women all the time who want to know, "Where is my husband? God let me down. How can I expect to have children, and I don't even have a husband yet?" I spend a lot of time praying and asking God for the right words to tell these women. All I can tell them is the same thing I tell women everywhere I minister: God is not a liar. He said He would give us the desires of our hearts if we would delight ourselves in Him (Ps. 37:4). Why it doesn't happen right away for some people? Frankly, I don't know. If you have a question about this, you are going to have to get in your prayer closet with God and find out for yourself. Spend time with Him. Pray in the Spirit and seek the Lord until you get your answer. The Lord is faithful; He is good, and He will honor His Word. I am a living witness of this. Research and meditate on these scriptures until they become alive to you, and then make them a part of your prayer life by confessing them daily: Psalm 37:4; Psalm 84:11; Mark 11:24; John 8:31–32; and John 15:7.

As I said before, God is not a liar. You are going to have to choose to believe what you are experiencing, or you are going to have to believe God's Word. If things are not going the way you want right now, you must continue with the Word. God will not let you down. He does not lie to us. If we are not living in the blessed state, it has to be something we are doing or maybe that the timing is just not right. We have to trust that we will have the manifestation of our prayers when it is the right time. We don't know what is ahead of us, but He does. He has done so much for us. The fact that

He sent Jesus to redeem us is enough for us to trust Him. Further, He has given us much assurance in the Bible that He will meet our needs and fulfill our desires if we live according to His Word.

You should not be somewhere by yourself, moping around feeling unfulfilled. There are too many people who feel unfulfilled in their lives. You don't need a mate to complete you for you to feel fulfilled, because you are complete in Jesus. Contribute to the good of society while you're trusting God for him or her. There are many people who need your help, and you can get joy from helping them. If you have a good job and are a good citizen there are things you can do to help other people who may not be as fortunate as you, such as volunteering in hospitals, orphanages, rest homes, and places like that. If you have money in abundance, you can give money, food, and clothing to people in need. Or you can be a tutor for people who are struggling in school. At our church, there are some college-age students who serve some of our younger members, and it is a tremendous blessing to many of our families. These young people give of their time and energy tutoring children who are having learning problems in school.

Of course, it goes without saying you should be involved with helping out at your church or giving time to some helps ministry. Every church and ministry I know of needs volunteers to help meet the needs of the people they are serving. At Crenshaw Christian Center, we have our Community Outreach Program (COP), in which we constantly need volunteers to disburse food and clothing and minister to people who need this kind of support. We need all kinds of help with that. We never have enough volunteers.

If you are not married, you can get involved in doing so much good in helping other people. We are saved to serve and saved to give. If you give and serve, you will forget about all the things that you don't have because you will be like Jesus, serving those who need our help. It can be therapy for you. Just look around you. There is just so much need. You don't have to be bored. If you get involved in helping somebody else, that is the greatest joy. It makes me so happy when I can do something for somebody. If you would look around and see the things that are needed and go and get involved with somebody else's life, you will find wonderful therapy for your own life.

That is what we are to do as Christians—meeting the needs of a desperate world gripped in sin and death. God only has us, those who are committed to living the Bible way, who will really stand up for Him, tell the truth, live right, and do what is right.

A friend of mine who happens to be white told me about her sister who was away attending a ministry training school. Her roommate, also white, came into the room where my friend's sister was listening to a tape by a Christian rap group. (Rap is mainly performed by black artists.) The roommate made a negative comment about her choice of music and used a derogatory name for black people. My friend said her sister was so outraged that before she knew it, she was screaming at her roommate about how wrong it was for anybody who was preparing for the ministry of the Lord Jesus Christ to say such a thing. She said to her roommate, "I came from

Fred Price's ministry, where everyone is treated the same. So I don't appreciate you saying something like that." I told her to tell her sister to get what she could from her studies at the school and, where she could, to minister to the individuals who would want to hear what she had to say.

Usually when somebody says something like that, they have never been around black people. They haven't realized yet that there are good and bad in every ethnic group. As the body of Christ, we have an obligation to minister to other Christians who have a prejudice problem. What is so good about being in the family of God is that we are all His children, and the Bible tells us He sees us and treats us all the same. Let us make up our minds that we are going to put off all those prejudices, hurts, complaints, criticisms, gripes, pride, arrogance, dislikes, and resentment toward other Christians. We need to put off self-centeredness, indifferences, and feelings of superiority—all these things come from the *old man*, and we need to put them off. We all need to come together and be sisters and brothers in the Lord, a family. God's family.

The Benefits of Being a Part of the Family

There is a lady at our church who has been a long-time member. She is well into her senior years now, but for many years she was a wonderful volunteer with our helps ministry and was a blessing to the ministry for a long time. She had been a member for more than twenty-one years when her husband died. After he passed, she had no one close to her to look out for her well-being. Her only child was killed when he was about eight years old, so here she was without a living soul left in her family. She said her husband was so ill that he should have died years ago, but he just held on as long as he could to try and stay here for her so she would not be alone. However, some of our church members pitched in to look out after her. She has involved herself so deeply in the church, helping wherever she could, that now she has so many adopted children looking out for her she can't count them all. That is what being a part of God's family is all about.

Sometimes it takes work to get along with other members of God's family. My children were just like other children when they were coming up. They were always fussing and arguing about something. In fact, we drove from Los Angeles to New York one year when Angela was about eleven years old and Cheryl was nine, and they fussed in the back seat during the whole trip. Fred and I told them we would never take them anywhere again. It takes time and effort to train your children in the way they should go. I remember a time that my two oldest daughters were at it again, and I simply got tired of it. I balled up my fists and went into the room and began hitting at both of them. I would hit this one and then that one, back and forward. I said, "You are going to love one another." They thought I had lost it, but today those girls are inseparable. And that is the way we are supposed to be in the body of Christ—loving one another—inseparable.

When Stephanie, our youngest daughter, came along, she didn't have any problems fighting with anyone. (Granted, there was no one to fight with.) Fred and I were just getting into traveling in ministry when she was growing up, so the two older girls helped in raising her. They were a wonderful help once I got them together. The three of them are still together today, and they love one another very much. We are called to fellowship with God and with one another. We are going to have to do it in heaven, so we should just as well get started now while we are on the Earth.

We are called to live for God and to fellowship with Him, and we have to do that. First John 1:3 says:

> That which we have seen and heard we declare to you, that you also may have fellowship with us; and truly our fellowship is with the Father and with His Son Jesus Christ.

We have to take that special time with Him and get to know Him. You may not feel like doing it, but you do it because God's Word says to do it. Spend time praying in the Spirit because that is the only way your spirit man is going to grow and be strong. Once you get into it, you will just love finding out what it is God has for you to do. Satan will do everything he can to keep you out of that Word, but that is the way you fellowship with the Father.

We are also called to live and fellowship with man.

> But the end of all things is at hand; therefore be serious and watchful in your prayers. And above all things have fervent love for one another, for "love will cover a multitude of sins." Be hospitable to one another without grumbling. As each one has received a gift, minister it to one another, as good stewards of the manifold grace of God.
>
> —1 Peter 4:7–10

> But if we walk in the light as He is in the light, we
> have fellowship with one another, and the blood of
> Jesus Christ His Son cleanses us from all sin.
>
> —1 JOHN 1:7

We are to minister to each other as we walk in the Word because we are family. That is how we learn about fellowship and how to treat one another.

The third thing we are called to do is to help save a world lost in sin, pain, and suffering. That is one big job, but we are called to do that. There is no end to serving, but it is wonderful to be able to serve one another and to serve God by ministering to the unsaved.

In Matthew 20:20, we have an account of when the mother of two of the disciples came to Jesus and wanted to know if her sons could sit on the right and left hand of Jesus when He came into His kingdom. Jesus responded to this question in verses 25–28:

> But Jesus called them to Himself and said, "You
> know that the rulers of the Gentiles lord it over
> them, and those who are great exercise authority
> over them. Yet it shall not be so among you; but
> whoever desires to become great among you, let
> him be your servant. And whoever desires to be
> first among you, let him be your slave—just as
> the Son of Man did not come to be served, but to
> serve, and to give His life a ransom for many."

It is very clear that serving is what we are to be doing. God has sent Jesus to serve. Luke 19:10 tells us why: "For the Son of Man has come to seek and to save that which was lost." Likewise, Jesus has sent us to serve for the same reason—to seek and save the lost. That is our number one purpose; that is why we are called to be His children. We are the body of Christ. He is looking to us to do His work, but we have to get ourselves together and walk in the high calling of God in order to do the work Jesus has called us to do. We have to get away from ourselves and all the things that would hinder us and keep us down.

CHAPTER 2

THE CALL TO SERVE

Through love serve one another.

—GALATIANS 5:13

E VERY BORN-AGAIN PERSON IS CALLED to servanthood. It is such a blessing to serve. To *serve* means "to wait on, to minister to."[1]

If you are not involved in serving somewhere in your church, ministry, community, or family, you should get involved. I don't know of any church that does not need some kind of help. In comparison to the total church membership, there are just too few people who actually serve in their churches. I know our church is no different from any other church, and we need help in so many ways. We have wonderful helps ministry workers who assist my husband and me in ministry. There is no way we could do all the work that needs to be done without their faithful service.

Paul says we are called to serve. In Galatians 5:13 he wrote:

> For you, brethren, have been called to liberty; only do not use liberty as an opportunity for the flesh, but through love serve one another.

We are called to liberty or freedom, but we are not to use that freedom as an opportunity to indulge our personal desires. In other words, we are not free to do whatever we feel like doing but rather to do what is right. Paul continued:

> For all the law is fulfilled in one word, even in this: "You shall love your neighbor as yourself." But if you bite and devour one another, beware lest you be consumed by one another!
>
> —GALATIANS 5:14–15

We, as believers, don't want to bite and devour one another like the people in the world do—fussing, fighting, and clawing for positions. The Bible tells us to walk in love and to love our neighbors as ourselves. If we do that, we will be in the will of God. That is why Jesus came here. He is the ultimate representative of love, and He left us an example to follow.

> He who loves his life will lose it, and he who hates his life in this world will keep it for eternal life. If anyone serves Me, let him follow Me; and where I am, there My servant will be also. If anyone serves Me, him My Father will honor.
>
> —JOHN 12:25–26

It is a blessing to serve the Lord. Jesus tells us that if we serve Him, His Father will honor us. Since Jesus is not here for us to serve Him directly, the way we serve Him is by serving one another with a sincere love.

Romans 12 offers believers important instruction regarding how to interact with people. Verses 9–13 tell us a number of ways in which we can get involved in serving our fellow believers.

> Let love be without hypocrisy. Abhor what is evil. Cling to what is good. Be kindly affectionate to one another with brotherly love, in honor giving preference to one another; not lagging in diligence, fervent in spirit, serving the Lord; rejoicing in hope, patient in tribulation, continuing steadfastly in prayer; distributing to the needs of the saints, given to hospitality.

The charge in verse 14 is more difficult:

> Bless those who persecute you; bless and do not curse.

I know this is hard for everybody to do, but we can do it because Jesus did it and told us to follow His example.

> Rejoice with those who rejoice, and weep with those who weep. Be of the same mind toward one another. Do not set your mind on high things, but associate with the humble. Do not be wise in your own opinion.
>
> —ROMANS 12:15–16

Sometimes we don't want to "be of the same mind" as other believers, but we are not acting in love when we become cliquish within certain groups. I know that even in churches there are little groups that cater to some people and exclude others. However, if we want to serve as Jesus said to serve, we have to be of the same mind toward one another without forming cliques.

> Repay no one evil for evil. Have regard for good things in the sight of all men. If it is possible, as much as depends on you, live peaceably with all men.
>
> —ROMANS 12:17–18

Notice that verse 18 says to be at peace with all men "if it is possible." There are times when it is not possible to do that. Don't feel guilty if you can't make a certain person like you or get along with a particular individual; some personalities simply clash with one another. You may not agree with some people all the time, but you still have the obligation to treat a brother and sister in Christ with respect and courtesy, because they represent Jesus as well. If someone rejects you, find someone else who needs to receive love from you. Stop beating your head against a wall trying to be around people who don't particularly like you. That is their problem, and they will have to deal with it. You don't have to worry about someone who is doing wrong to you. You just keep on doing good, and God will take care of that situation.

> Beloved, do not avenge yourselves, but rather give place to wrath; for it is written, "Vengeance is Mine, I will repay," says the Lord. Therefore "If your enemy is hungry, feed him; If he is thirsty, give him a drink; For in so doing you will heap coals of fire on his head." Do not be overcome by evil, but overcome evil with good.
>
> —ROMANS 12:19–21

All these verses are self-explanatory. If we would take heed to what they tell us to do, we would have no problems whatsoever in showing love toward our neighbors or anyone else and we would be right with the Lord.

Acts 10:38 says that Jesus went about doing good and healing all who were oppressed of the devil. We can be like Him because there is always somebody we can minister to, and that is what we ought to be doing wherever and whenever we can. A lot of times we want to go and serve the popular people, and most times, they don't even need our service. We are not to be partial to the people we like or the people we like to be around. Instead, let God open the door for you and show you where you can meet a need.

The Importance of Being Like-Minded

> Therefore if there is any consolation in Christ, if any comfort of love, if any fellowship of the Spirit, if an affection and mercy, fulfill my joy by being like-minded, having the same love, being of one accord, of one mind. Let nothing be done through selfish ambition or conceit, but in lowliness of mind let each esteem others better than himself. Let each of you look out not only for his own interests, but also for the interests of others.
>
> —PHILIPPIANS 2:1–4

We should be obedient to what Paul tells us in these verses. We need to be concerned about the interests of our brothers and sisters and not just think about ourselves. As we do this, the blessings of the Lord will come. It starts first at home with your family. If you don't get yourself together in your own life and with your own family, it will be very difficult for you to go out and share—with any conviction—about the Christian life and Jesus.

You need to have a personal relationship with Jesus and know Him in reality for yourself. What has He done for you, and what will He do? You won't know these things about Jesus unless you first act in faith and believe for Him to move in your life. You have to believe that He is moving in your life even when you don't see it. If you can learn that, you will have victory no matter what you're going through. Then people will look at you and say, "How can she be so happy while she is going through all of this?" You can be a witness that God is real when you act like you know you can go through anything because Jesus is with you and He will bring you through, no matter what the situation or how long it takes. Our walk with Christ is not just for us, but it is also to show Jesus to the world.

A lot of Christians will start out using their faith when they are going through the challenge, but then their emotions or the trauma of what they are going through will get them off track and cause them to lose their focus on the Lord. Then they start making all kinds of terrible decisions that will haunt them for months and sometimes years. You can always use your faith and make the decision to get out of situations that you have gotten into, but you have to stay focused on God. You can't look at what you see. If I had looked at circumstances when I was diagnosed with cancer and needed hip and then knee surgery, I don't know if I would still be here today. But I refused to look at what I saw, the sickness and disease. Instead, I looked at what I believed, and I stood firm on God's Word.

The Importance of Being a Witness for Jesus

We can start being a witness for the Lord right in our own homes. If you are a married woman, you can serve by putting love into action by following Ephesians 5:22, which says, "Wives, submit to your own husbands, as to the Lord." Most people don't like the word *submit*. However, submission is an act of love, especially when you do it as unto the Lord. Submission doesn't mean taking an inferior position or role. It is just that God has ordained it that somebody has to be the head, and somebody has to follow. God placed women in the position to be submissive to their husbands, who are, or should be, the heads of the households. The rank is: God the Father, Jesus Christ, the Holy Spirit, then man, woman, and the children.

I have never understood why some women want to be the "man" of the house when there is a man in the home capable of fulfilling that role. We women don't need to do that. If the husband is not quite the head of the house, he should be. If you will submit like the Word says, God will take care of the husband. So many times we try to figure out how God is going to work. If we don't wait on Him and instead do things our way, we mess things up. When we let God do it, things end up much better. All of it is by faith first. You have to learn to commit your spouse to the Lord, because nobody has the perfect spouse. No woman should expect her husband to be perfect, because she is not perfect.

Unfortunately, some of us want our spouses to be right on in everything and in every way. It is not going to happen. When you get married, you start out just like a baby—a baby marriage. You have to give and take. Now, this does not mean that you have to put up with or take all kinds of abuse, but you do have to give and take and allow your spouse to grow up. Ephesians 5:33 says, "Nevertheless let each one of you in particular so love his wife as himself, and the wife see that she respects her husband." The part I want to emphasize is that the wife respects her husband. Some women question this saying and ask, "Why should I have to respect him?"

At a wedding I attended, the minister was reading the marriage vows, and when he got to the part where it talked about the wife reverencing her husband, the young woman said, "I don't want to say that. Why should I have to do that?" Well, you can see that the marriage was not getting off to a good start. The wife's respect for her husband is a part of marriage, at least a Christian marriage. Like I said, submission doesn't mean that the wife has to do absolutely anything the husband tells her to; God doesn't want us to do anything that would violate our conscience or our Christian witness.

Christian women can serve our sisters in Christ by giving them Bible-based information. Women who are being abused should know that God does not expect them to submit to the abuse of an abusive husband. If you are in a situation like that—and many Christian women are—know that your body is the temple of the Holy Spirit, and He did not provide you salvation so that you could live beat up, whipped, and defeated. God does not expect you to stay in an abusive situation. Hebrews 13:4 says, "Marriage is honorable among all, and the bed undefiled; but fornicators and adulterers God will judge." Some people take this verse out of context and think that the phrase *the bed undefiled* means you can do just anything in marriage that the body feels like doing. Sometimes the wife doesn't want to perform certain sexual acts, or sometimes the husband does not want to do those things that are perverse.

I counsel with women all the time whose husbands want to have oral sex. They say, "Well, you know, the Bible says marriage is honorable and the bed undefiled, so my husband wants to have oral sex. Should I do that?" I have to tell them that this scripture is not condoning oral sex. What it means is that it is God-ordained for married people to have sex with their own spouses. It doesn't mean to do all the perverted stuff that people get in bondage to. Believe me, in my years of counseling couples I have learned a lot of weird stuff Christians do, like looking at pornography while having sex or just before having sex with their spouses in order to get a bigger thrill. Some women have even brought me some of the movies they watch with their husbands. Oh, my goodness! I don't know how in the world Christians get into this kind of thing.

You could not possibly think God would expect you to submit to looking at things like that. If you are engaged in a situation in which your conscience (which is the voice of your spirit) is telling you not to continue, you are going to have to be strong enough in the Lord to take your stand and believe God will impress it upon your spouse not to deal in that kind of thing. Until then, for your own piece of mind you are going to have to do what you know to be biblically right.

I have told this story before, but I'm going to tell it again because there is a point I want to make. When Fred and I got married, I didn't know he didn't like going to church. When we were dating he went to church with me every single Sunday, and he would come to the house with me after church for dinner. Because my family was so big, my parents had to provide food that was filling, as well as good. We ate the same thing for dinner every Sunday: okra with lima beans, rice, and fried chicken. After we got married Fred told me, "Don't ever give me okra again, and I'm not going to church anymore on Sundays because I want to play baseball on Sunday mornings." I was crushed, but I had to make a decision. I was born again in the Baptist church and loved God, and I was not going to let anyone take that away from me. I was newly married, and I didn't know what Fred would do.

That is where a lot of women make a mistake; they get scared and think the man might leave. Let him leave! He is not stronger than God. You can live without a man, but you can't live without God.

So, Fred started playing baseball on Sunday mornings and I continued to go to church. I believe we are where we are today because I took that stand. If you take a stand that is right and the man really wants to be right, God can work with that man. On the other hand, if you don't do what is right, God doesn't have anything to work with. The Bible tells us that if the wife will set the example by her godly conduct, she can win the husband over to God's side. (See 1 Peter 3:1.)

I didn't know what Fred was going to do when I told him I intended to continue going to church, but I was not going to live without God. Being in church was precious to me from the time I first heard about God, and I was not going to stop going because Fred didn't want to go. I said to myself, "Well, this man does not know any better, but I do. I'm going to church, and he can do whatever he wants to do." I didn't know if he would leave me or not, but I knew I needed God more than I needed him. I started doing what I was supposed to do.

I went on to church, and he ended up following me because he wanted to find out where I was going and what I was into. He got trapped following me and he ended up getting saved. What a blessing our salvation has been to our marriage. I hate to think what would have happened if I had given in to what he wanted to do. Where would we be today? God will honor the person who is right. You wives have to be strong in your right decisions and not think that you have to submit to any old thing just because the Bible says to submit to your husbands.

I know some men can become violent when they can't have their way. You are going to have to trust God to protect you, and I believe He will. However, if He has given you a way to get out of that situation, then you need to get out of there. Don't stay there and let somebody beat up on you.

I used to say to women, "I believe I could take verbal abuse as long as my husband wasn't physically beating me." I have recently had to retract my statement. I have never gone through this kind of abuse—Fred fusses, but he has never been verbally abusive—but some women have told me that verbal, emotional abuse is worse than physical abuse. They said that once your spouse hits you, breaks your nose, or does something like that, you can heal. Mental abuse, though, just stays there eating at you and tearing you up on the inside. After hearing such comments I realized all kinds of abuse are bad.

If you got yourself in an abusive situation, you are going to have to take action to get yourself out of it, with God's help. Some denominations claim that the scripture that says, "What therefore God hath put together, let no man put asunder [separate]" (Mark 10:9, KJV) means that you can't get a divorce or get remarried. My answer to that is, "Yes, if God put you together, let nobody separate you. Unfortunately, God didn't put a lot of people together. They put themselves together." We are not perfect, and if you made a mistake by putting yourself together with whomever who is abusing you, you and God are going to have to figure how to get you out. God does not want His children misused or abused. Your body is the temple of the Holy Spirit—the very place where God dwells—and He doesn't want a beat-up temple. Just like you don't want to stay in a beat-up house, He does not want to stay in a beat-up temple. You have to make the decision as to what to do about the situation. I do believe a wife can and should love her husband through the adjustment period they will go through when they are first married. People have to be trained and grow in marriage. But abusive behavior is a different matter.

When our children were growing up, my husband and I never argued in front of them. They knew that their father loved me and I loved and respected him. As they grew up, they found out that nobody agrees all the time with everything. Today, it doesn't matter what they hear because I have trained them. The Bible says that the older women are to train the younger women in marriage. Now that they have husbands, they know how to act when they experience the things all couples experience in marriage, including disagreements.

My girls will call me from time to time for advice, and they can tell you I never take sides with them. Sometimes there's hardly enough money or they made wrong decisions and bought stuff they should not have bought, and they are suffering from it; Fred and I did that when we first got married. All I do is give them the Word. I listen to them and I say, "Well, that is just something you will have to live through. You can live through the situations that young marriages have to face." It takes patience, but you can live through it. We have to learn how to put the flesh under. Personally, I don't care about being the one to win an argument. I just get in agreement real quick, because it doesn't matter who wins, if we are one in Christ.

If something hurt their feelings, I will tell them, "Well, you know, you shouldn't let that hurt you because the Bible tells you to reckon yourselves to be dead. If you are dead, how can he hurt your feelings?" When I said this to one of our girls, she responded, "That is all good and well, but this sister wants to rise from the dead!" After a little while she came to me with this other revelation she thought she had. She said, "Mom, I know you said to act like you're dead, but you are not really dead. You are really feeling everything." I had a very simple answer for her, the same answer I have for everybody: "We don't walk by how we feel; we walk by faith."

Your faith will see you through these little situations. I bet that I have gone through everything every young married person has ever gone through. I made it, and I am no different than anyone else as far as having to go through things. There were many times when there wasn't enough money, enough clothes—enough of anything. However, if you dare to stand

and believe God's Word, God will bring you through these hard times and put you on top.

In the meantime, don't go around complaining and crying to your friends and family members. This is just not good. It's the worse thing you can do to your spouse, particularly if he or she is not saved. Unsaved people see things differently than saved people do, or I should say, than saved people who know the Word do. Some of our church members have counseling sessions with me and they will tell me things about their husbands. That's different. They know I am not going to go and tell their business. Our pastoral staff does a lot of counseling, and we are bound to keep what is told to us confidential unless a civil law is broken. (We are bound to report to the law enforcement agency any felony laws, like child abuse or murder, that are violated.) I might use someone's situation as an illustration, but I never use names and am careful to protect the individuals' identities so no one knows whom I am talking about. I like sharing testimonies because a lot of people have gone through similar situations, but I always make sure the people involved are protected.

One lady I was counseling told me a lot of things about her husband, so I said, "Okay, now you have told me, so you don't need to go and tell anyone else about those matters." Later I found out she was telling everybody who would listen to her about her situation. Now when the husband comes around her friends or family he feels like he is about as big as a grasshopper because of the things she has told them about him. After the two of you make up and you are all lovey-dovey again, your family and friends are thinking, "Well, why in the world are you staying with him if he treated you badly?"

My advice is to keep your mouth shut. Let God work your marriage situation out, and walk by faith.

Communication, talking to each other about various matters, is vital for the success of a marriage. I once counseled a wife who told me that she and her husband had never talked about how many children they would have. If you don't get in agreement on this matter beforehand, a child will come along that you were not expecting and it may cause problems. In her case, the husband was very upset when his wife got pregnant and blamed her for the pregnancy, as if he didn't have anything to do with it. She, in turn, told everybody how her husband felt, though I advised her not to do that. I told her he would get over it, and that when that child came he would be so happy.

When I was forty-four years old I suddenly came up expecting. It was a shock to me and a bigger shock to my husband. He wasn't ready, and neither was I. We thought we were finished having children. Angela was twenty-two; Cheryl, nineteen; and Stephanie was eleven. Cheryl and Stephanie were still living at home, but Angela was married. When I came from the doctor, Cheryl said you would have thought I had committed a crime or something. Cheryl said I came into her room, closed the door, and whispered, "Cheryl, I'm pregnant." She said, "Well, is it Dad's?" Cheryl is like that. You have to be around her to know the comments she can come up with off the top of her head. I said, "I'm too old to be having a baby." She said, "You're not too old, because if you were too old you wouldn't be having it." And then she said, "You and Dad should be ashamed of yourselves. You are good parents. Why wouldn't you want to have another child?"

Her father said, "I know I'm a good parent. That's why I don't want to have anymore kids. It costs something to raise children." By the way Fred was acting and what he was saying, you would have thought I got pregnant by myself. Fred vents when he is upset, and when he is venting he doesn't mean what he says. He's done that since I've known him. Once the initial shock and disappointment was over and Fred found out it was going to be a boy, he was on cloud nine.

Now suppose I had come to the congregation—which was very large by this time—and to our television audience with my head down and feeling and looking all bad because of what Fred had been saying. Wouldn't that have been a great example for the church? But the congregation never knew a thing. I was the most wonderful forty-five-year-old pregnant woman I could be, and nobody ever knew about the morning sickness and all the other discomforts a pregnant woman goes through, especially a pregnant woman my age. You don't have to let negativity come out of your mouth. You don't have to be like little children or teenagers always wanting to speak their minds.

It is not that hard to live with a husband and to put up with the things that every married couple has to put up with. If you know anything about Fred Price, you know that he is very particular about certain things. He has a schedule for just about everything he does because he likes everything just so. I often hear, "Don't break into my schedule," or, "Don't talk to me while I'm doing this." He does have a very busy schedule, and he tries his best to stay on the schedule he has set for himself. We get up at seven o'clock every morning, except

Sunday morning, when we get up at five o'clock because of our church service.

Because of Fred's morning routine, no one can say anything to him between seven o'clock and nine thirty in the morning, nor does he take phone calls between those hours. He prays for one hour and a half and then he reads his Bible. He also fixes our breakfast—we eat a variety of fruit, which he cuts up for us; that is his job every morning. While he is cutting the fruit and eating, we do not talk because he is meditating on what he has read in the Bible or he is still studying. When he has finished eating and studying the Bible, he goes into the bedroom to start getting dressed.

As you can imagine, once in a while we have to say something to him. One time, Cheryl and I were working on something to help him at the church. Cheryl called to see if I would ask him something she needed to know, and Fred began fussing about interrupting his schedule. She could hear him over the phone and said, "Oh, Mom, just forget it." I know my husband very well, so I don't let these kinds of reactions bother me. I said, "Oh, no. We're not going to forget it; we are going to do it this way." All of a sudden, this man who is so busy and can't talk on the telephone and doesn't have time to say anything to anybody says, "No, you can't do it that way." I said, "Oh, yes we can; you are not in this." There was nothing he could say. When I tell this story he just laughs. Fred realizes that he has to be bothered sometimes, because if we can't get to him, we are going to do things our way. In this situation, we did do it our way, and it was a blessing to him.

You cannot let your feelings get hurt to the point where you don't tell your husband what you know he needs to hear, no matter what he says. The wife is her husband's helper. God ordained it that way, so you cannot have your feelings on your fingertips. Your responsibility as a wife is to tell your husband what you feel or sense is right. Then if he does not agree—and sometimes he won't—you are going to have to let it go. When I know I am right, I don't worry about it because I know God will minister to him. I don't have to fall on the floor and have a fit in that little whiney voice that men hate. While you are doing all of that the Holy Spirit can't talk to your husband because all he will be able to hear is you complaining and whining. However, if you will give it to God, God will talk to him and minister to his heart. I always tell the Lord, "OK, God, You know that is a good idea, so you talk to him." Sure enough, God will talk to him. Then Fred will do exactly what I said we should do. Now, I'm not saying that I am right all the time. That is why we need one another. When the wife is weak in some area the husband can be strong for the both of them, particularly in raising children.

Called to Serve One Another as Parents

I remember when Frederick, our son, was seventeen years of age. He had just learned how to drive, and he liked to be out late. Stephanie also liked to stay out late when she was that age. When she and Frederick got to be about sixteen or seventeen, they didn't want us to tell them what time to come home. They just wanted to be out. They were not getting into anything; they just felt more grown-up being out with their friends.

The college town of Westwood out by UCLA was very popular with college students and teenagers when Stephanie, our youngest daughter, was growing up. When I asked her what she and her friends were doing all that time hanging around there she said, "You can come with me, Mom, and see what goes on and what we do." I did go once, and all they did was walk up and down the streets, talking and laughing with the other kids. It was very tiring, but at least I saw what she was into. It was nothing to worry about.

Even after I saw what they were doing, when it got to be a certain time at night Satan would start shooting thoughts into my mind. My mind is no different than any other mother's mind. I had to learn to close the mind off, otherwise thoughts would come, such as "they could have gotten into some kind of trouble; there could be an accident"—all kinds of thoughts. I remember one particular time Frederick was out shopping around Christmas, not long after he had started driving. Stephanie and her husband had gone on vacation, and she had asked him to come by her house and feed her goldfish. It was midnight when I got a call from Frederick. He had run out of gas. My heart dropped. I thought, "Oh, he is just a baby, and he is out there by himself in this big city. Oh, my goodness!" Actually, he was parked in front of Stephanie's house.

I pray for my children on a daily basis. I pray for their protection, that they have wisdom, that they have the knowledge to make right decisions, and that God's angels are encamped around them to keep them from destruction. I pray this all the time for my kids, but still you can do something wrong, and you have to pay the price. That Christmas, Frederick had let himself run out of gas. There was no excuse for it because he had a credit card. He could have bought gas when he needed to. Even if he had run out of money, he could still have bought gas. Anyway, he was negligent, and he ran out of gas; so he called me. Naturally, children know to call Momma because she will take care of everything. Frederick told me he was out of gas and wanted me to come pick him up.

Fred was lying in bed beside me when Frederick called. He turned to me and said, "Where is Freddy?" I told him he was at Stephanie's house, and he had run out of gas. I explained that I was going to get up and go get him. Fred said, "You're not going anywhere." I said, "Well, I'm not going to rest. I can't rest knowing he's out there." He replied, "If you go out there, you stay out there with him." So I said, "Well, I guess I won't go." He said, "You tell Frederick to go inside Stephanie's house and stay the night. He can get up in the morning and walk to the gas station two blocks away, get a can of gas, and put the gas in the car. Then he can drive home." I had to admit that his solution was better than mine. I bet Freddy will never run out of gas again. Thank God Frederick had a father who was strong enough to make that decision and not get emotional like his mother did.

The Body of Christ Needs to Serve One Another

I have seen situations in our church where a family seemed perfectly happy and all of a sudden you look up and the husband is gone; he has gotten on drugs or alcohol, or some other kind of addiction. Sometimes we find out that a wife has left her husband for another man, leaving behind the husband and children. I have seen it both ways—the husband is gone or the wife is gone. However, it is more often the husband who has left the family.

Sometimes Christians get into trouble and they don't know what to do. They feel so bad about the situations they are in that they will leave the church. It is amazing how people think that everybody knows their business. The devil feeds the thought to their minds that everybody knows what they are going through and they begin to feel low. Eventually their self-esteem just goes out the window.

This one family in particular began as beautiful Christians, then the husband got into all kinds of things. He ended up on drugs and started running around on his wife. She eventually had to get out of the marriage, but she was devastated. Her emotions got so messed up she ran from the place where she needed to be the most—her church. She got involved with another man, and when I finally got an opportunity to talk to her, she said she didn't know how she ever got into that situation. The guy wasn't even a Christian, and he took advantage of her left and right. She told me, "Sometimes you just can't think properly when you are going through so much stuff and you have been put down like I was. Your self-esteem is so low. You don't realize what you are into and how far your emotions have gotten you off track. Even though in your head you know what the Word of God says, somehow you won't go there."

This is where a lot of us in the body of Christ can help to serve our brothers and sisters who have gone the wrong way. We can be there to pray with them, talk to them, and encourage them to get back in church and back with God.

It was only after the woman I spoke with had gotten into this situation with this other man, who turned out to be worse than her husband had been, that she finally came to me and said, "You have got to help me. I just need some help. I need to be back in church, and I need you to help me get back." She said that the man beat her and abused her emotionally and mentally, always playing mind games on her. She was a total wreck when she finally came to me and asked for help. After hearing this woman's story God gave me the concept for our Women Who Care meetings. Women Who Care is now a part of our ministry to women at Crenshaw Christian Center. The women meet twice a month on Sunday evenings to hear other women share their testimonies and pray with one another, as well as to fellowship and build strong bonds of sisterhood. It has been very successful in helping women understand who they are in Christ and how to be overcomers when going through a difficult time. It is a good opportunity for women to work together.

We have to be committed to what the Lord is leading us to do. We cannot be gossiping and talking about other people's business or taking advantage of a person when she is down. As the body of Christ, we should want to be there to help a brother or sister to get out of those traps Satan has set for them, not just for their own benefit but for the glory of God. This is called spiritual mentoring, parenting, or nurturing. If we want to be a part of this process, we should heed Titus 2:1–8.

> But as for you, speak the things which are proper for sound doctrine: that the older men be sober, reverent, temperate, sound in faith, in love, in patience; the older women likewise, that they be reverent in behavior, not slanderers, not given to much wine, teachers of good things...
>
> —TITUS 2:1–3

These are the qualities needed for mentoring, nurturing, or teaching spiritual principles. Notice that it says the women are required to have the same virtues as the men. They are not to be gossipers, speaking evil of people and running them down.

> ...that they admonish the young women to love their husbands, to love their children, to be discreet, chaste, homemakers, good, obedient to their own husbands, that the word of God may not be blasphemed. Likewise, exhort the young men to be sober-minded, in all things showing yourself to be a pattern of good works; in doctrine showing integrity, reverence, incorruptibility [in other words, of strong spiritual character that cannot be corrupted], sound speech that cannot be condemned, that one who is an opponent may be ashamed, having nothing evil to say of you.
>
> —TITUS 2:4–8

That last part means that people may talk about you, but it's your job to guard your conduct so that their slander isn't true.

Women helping women is a commandment from God. You may not be called to a public ministry, but you are called to minister. Equipping women or training women in spiritual matters is an important part of the responsibility of spiritually mature women. If you are not serving in any other place in the church, there is a place where you can serve and minister to the needs of women. Christian women who may be going through a rough time should not be out there by themselves thinking that nobody cares about them. They can come and be built up in the church until their spirit is strong and they can go on with their lives. It is up to the older women to minister to the younger women. You might have to start in your own home. The Bible tells us that Jesus called twelve men. There were not any women among those twelve, yet women ministered to Jesus all the time. They followed Him, they ministered to Him financially, and they provided Him with hospitality. All of these are areas where we can get involved.

The Great Commission was given to women as well as to men. The single woman, the wife, the grandmother, and the widow are all called to go and be a witness for Jesus. Going does not necessarily mean leaving home and family, but it does mean making yourself available to serve wherever, whenever, and however the Lord directs. Many times the greatest position of influence in fulfilling the Great Commission is not a visible and public one. Sadly, some women don't want to be involved in a one-on-one ministry because they want to be seen and noticed. In my opinion, the most rewarding ministry is not visible and public. Women can serve in their own homes by influencing their husbands for good and disciplining their own children. As that familiar saying goes, "The hand that rocks the cradle is the hand that rules the world." Women have an essential position in the home.

Hannah had influence on her son Samuel. (See 1 Samuel 1 and 2.) She had been barren all of her married life. She prayed to God to have a child, and when He granted her wish she gave the child back to God for His service. Samuel was the last judge of Israel, and he was an outstanding and gifted prophet. He anointed the first two kings of Israel. What an effect his mother had on the nation of Israel, all because of her commitment to serve God through her son.

We Can Serve Through Hospitality

There are so many ways to be of service in the church. In Romans 12:13 Paul talks about hospitality. The scripture says it entails "distributing to the needs of the saints" and being "given to hospitality." Hospitality is the practice of welcoming, sheltering, and feeding others with no thought of personal gain. The resources that need to be available for the ministry of hospitality include food, money, time, energy, creativity, and most of all, love. There are some people who have the gift of hospitality. Like every other gift, you have to recognize the call for this type of service and be willing to make yourself available to answer the call. Food and clothing outreach programs such as our Community Outreach Program (COP) are excellent ways to minister to people's physical needs while they are learning how to apply the Word to their lives.

It is not God's perfect plan that anyone be dependent upon such outreach programs. God desires that all of His children walk in victory over every circumstance and that all of our needs be met. However, the fact is that some Christians, for whatever reason, are unable to apply the Word to their lives immediately, so God uses the church to help meet the needs of His children. That is why programs like our COP are important outreach ministry tools for churches to use. If your church does not have an active outreach program, there are many other organizations that need volunteers to work with them in reaching out to the needy. In addition to our own outreach program, we also financially assist other ministries that provide food, shelter, and clothing. I encourage you to join with one of them. You will find the benefits very rewarding. You can't imagine how therapeutic it is to get involved in something like that. It is a tremendous blessing for one and all.

I sincerely believe that no Christian will ever really be able to enjoy their relationship with the Lord Jesus Christ until they get involved with serving one another. Christians need to get involved and encourage one another with love. That is when you will really enjoy your Christian life. Once we did a survey of the church members who had been with the church at least one year to determine how many of them would be interested in getting involved with the helps ministry. I could not believe how many single men stood up to volunteer. Actually, there were more single men between the ages of twenty-five and forty-five who said they wanted to help than women! I challenged them to get involved in what was going on in the church.

Service Among the Singles of the Church

There are so many opportunities at church for singles to serve. I know that at Crenshaw Christian Center there is always a need for single women to be surrogate sisters to our teenagers and seniors through our Big Sisters program. Sometimes teenage girls need someone they can talk to who is spiritually mature and will guide them in the things of the Lord. Likewise, our seniors are always looking for someone who can assist them with a variety of needs, such as taking them to doctor's appointments, grocery shopping, or even just out to lunch. If you have the finances, this can be an excellent way of ministering to those who may not have the money to go out to lunch on their own. If nothing else, it can certainly get your mind off the fact that you don't have a husband and your biological clock is ticking away.

We also have a Big Brothers program where the older men minister to the needs of boys who do not have fathers at home. The men who serve in this program have their acts together and are good role models for the boys to follow. We cannot get enough workers for this program, but the men who are involved, both single and married, are committed to the boys and serve them faithfully. They have different activities where the boys get a chance to fellowship with other Christian boys. They take them to baseball and football games, as well as other sports outings. Once they took sixty of the boys from the church to a baseball game, and some of the spectators around them complimented them on their good behavior and neat appearance.

I pray all the time, "Lord, let the people serving at our church be of right motive and mind. Let them have the right heart, and protect us from those who don't." Honesty and integrity have a lot to do with our Christian walk, especially our service. Colossians 3:23 tells us, "And whatever you do, do it heartily, as to the Lord and not to men." In other words, whatever you do or say, do it as unto the Lord. If you can't do it as unto the Lord, then don't do it. This is how we train ourselves to be people of integrity, honesty, and character.

I want to caution you against serving so that you can get help yourself. Go with an attitude that you are going to be a giver to the Lord through serving your spiritual brothers and sisters. When you serve with the right heart God will give you whatever you need to make your life fruitful and fulfilling. Don't think that God doesn't know where you are. He knows where you are and He knows your need. Hebrews 6:10 says, "For God is not unjust to forget your work and labor of love which you have shown toward His name, in that you have ministered to the saints, and do minister." God will be there for you. He will bless you, and He will give you the return on your giving. Take it from me: there is no greater life than working with the Lord to serve one another.

CHAPTER 3

GROWING IN GODLINESS

Pursue righteousness, godliness, faith, love,
patience, gentleness.

—1 TIMOTHY 6:11

GODLINESS MEANS TO BE MORE like God by living a holy life in our thoughts, actions, and deeds. Holiness is living the godly life.

I pray the following prayer daily for the congregation at our church. It is based on 1 Peter 2:2, Ephesians 1:17–18, and Ephesians 3:16–19.

> *That we would continue to desire the sincere milk of the Word, so that we may grow thereby; that we may grow in the grace and knowledge of Jesus Christ; that we have the Spirit of wisdom and revelation in the knowledge of Him; that the eyes of our understanding will be enlightened; that we might make right decisions in life; and that we may be blameless in His presence.*
>
> *That we will be strengthened with all might by*

His Spirit in the inner man; that Christ might dwell in our hearts by faith; and that we, being rooted and grounded in love, will be able to comprehend with all the saints what is the breadth, the length, height, and depth; and to know, that is to experience the love of Christ, which passes knowledge, and be filled with all of His fullness to the praise, glory, and honor of His name. That we might represent Him from the ministries of Crenshaw Christian Center in word and in deed, by precept and example; that we live godly lives; that we will walk in the Spirit in order not to fulfill the lust of the flesh; and that we walk in divine health, divine prosperity, and that all of our needs are met.

I pray this prayer all the time for the members of our church. We might not see every aspect of it in manifestation just yet, but we still pray what the Word says, believing that we will see the total manifestation some day. That is how faith works.

I believe that the body of Christ will come into the fullness of the knowledge of Jesus Christ and that we will live the life He has provided for us. The way we do that is to make up our minds that we are going to grow in godliness and be more like Him. John 14:9 records that Jesus told his disciples, "He who has seen Me has seen the Father." If we want to grow in God, we need to know about Jesus, and we have His Word to show us the things that He did. I read the Gospel of John over and over again to get a fuller knowledge of God because that is where Jesus reveals the Father clearly.

Godly living means leading a self-controlled life. In order
to do that, we have to make rules for ourselves that exem-
plify godly conduct. In the following pages I will be repeating
some of the scriptures I used in previous chapters, but I want
to expound on these scriptures a little more. In Titus 2:1–5,
the apostle Paul gives instructions to Titus, a young minister,
concerning his position as a minister of the gospel, and
instructions for the church under his care. Verse 1 reads:

> But as for you, speak the things which are proper
> for sound doctrine.

Sound doctrine means healthy, uncorrupt biblical
teaching. Today we would say, "Sound doctrine is teaching
and preaching the uncompromising Word."

> That the older men be sober, reverent, temperate,
> sound in faith, in love, in patience.
>
> —TITUS 2:2

When it says *older men*, it means older men in the church
who were not necessarily ministers. To be sober means to
be circumspect and self-controlled.[1] The word *reverent*
means "behavior that is dignified, honorable, decent, worthy
of respect." *Temperate* means "to be marked by moderation
as keeping or held within limits, not excessive, moderation
in indulgence of appetite or desire." Notice that all of these
virtues have to do with self-control.

Hebrews 11:6 says it is impossible to please God without
faith. First John 5:4 tells us, "For whatever is born of God
overcomes the world. And this is the victory that has over-

come the world—our faith." We need to continually exercise our faith in the things we are learning, because faith and the Word are synonymous. Romans 10:17 says, "Faith comes by hearing, and hearing by the word of God." We need to continue to hear the Word taught, so that our minds will not grow lax. That is what has happened to a lot of Christians; their minds grew lax. The Word didn't have a chance to get into their spirits so that it could become real to them. You have to hear the Word over and over so it can get into your spirit. It has always been the aim of Crenshaw Christian Center to teach God's people sound, faith-based doctrine.

Going back to the list of requirements for older men in Titus 2:2, being *sound in love* means understanding that love is not a feeling. Love is giving. Love is doing. Love is caring. Love is long-suffering. The final trait, patience, is the ability to wait, to put up with, and to persevere.

These instructions were given to the older men so that they could be examples for the young men to follow. These young men thereby would learn to be men of character, good husbands, and good fathers.

After describing suggestions for the behavior of the older men, Paul lists some qualities that were to be hallmarks of the older women's lives.

> The older women likewise, that they be reverent in behavior, not slanderers, not given to much wine, teachers of good things.
>
> —TITUS 2:3

We already covered what reverent means. The act of slander means "the utterance of false charges, or misrepresentation that defames and damages another's reputation."[2] In modern terms, when Paul tells Titus to ensure that the older women are not slanderers, he is saying that they should not be false accusers or malicious gossipers. Sadly, there are just too many Christians who are involved in gossip. Women seem to be guiltier of this than men, but it is something that we Christians really need to be careful about.

Paul suggested that Titus admonish the women not to consume too much wine. In biblical times, water was scarce and of poor quality for drinking, so the people drank wine often as a substitute for water. This is not an excuse for us to drink wine today. In fact, at Crenshaw Christian Center we require all of our employees and helps ministry workers to abstain from alcohol of any kind, as well as from smoking. There are a lot of people who start out drinking wine or beer, but they become alcoholics later. Our family just made up our minds that we as a family would not drink any kind of alcoholic beverages. We always want to be an example of godly living.

Titus 2:3 also says that the older women are to be teachers of good things. We older women need to work on this so that we can be examples to the younger women and all other young people. We can teach what it means to be godly women by the example we set. In addition to using our actions as a teaching tool, we should speak wisely, passing on valuable knowledge and advice, such as what Paul suggests in verse 4:

That they admonish the young women to love
their husbands, to love their children.

Now that is a very interesting statement: admonish the
young women to love their husbands and children. You
would think that loving one's husband and children would
be automatic, but evidently it is not. When people first get
married, they think that it is all about feelings and having
fun. After a while, they find out that they have responsibili-
ties that may not be so enjoyable. To love your husband and
children means you take care of them and their needs. This
means cooking, cleaning, washing, helping with homework,
training, disciplining, and all the other things that go with
being a wife and a mother. I know in these modern days
when so many wives work outside the home, many times
the husband has to fix the food and help out with household
chores; and if the wife works, he should. However, I know of
some women who don't work who tell their husbands to fix
their own food. Ladies, the Bible still says the same thing that
it said in Paul's time. If we follow the rules set by the Bible, we
will have good results and will live more peaceful and harmo-
nious married lives.

As I said before, love is not just a feeling. Love is caring,
love is doing, and love is training. Children have to be trained
to be what God would have them to be, and it is the parents'
responsibility to make them do what they need to do.
Sometimes you feel like giving up, but as a parent you have to
be willing to stay there and do whatever is necessary to keep
your children on the right track. It is especially hard to deal
with kids when they become teenagers because they think

they are grown when they are not. I used to say, "Let's freeze them from twelve to nineteen years of age!" But we can't do that, so we have to stay with them and train them.

Parents have to train their children; otherwise, their kids will just go their own way, and when they are grown they won't know how to do a thing around the house. Just before Frederick was born we finally got to the place where we could afford a housekeeper to help me with household chores several days a week. When Frederick was still little I began trying to train him to make his bed and to keep his room clean. On the days the housekeeper would come, Frederick would not make his bed or straighten up his room. I asked him, "Why didn't you make your bed today?" He answered, "Well, isn't Anna coming?" I said, "Yes, Anna is coming today, but she is not coming to make your bed. When you get grown, you may not have a maid to come and help you. I was forty-five years old when I got a maid, so you've got a few more years to go."

Paul had more suggestions regarding what older women should teach the younger women.

> To be discreet, chaste, homemakers, good, obedient to their own husbands, that the word of God might not be blasphemed.
>
> —TITUS 2:5

The word *discreet* means "having or showing discernment or good judgment or good conduct, especially in speech."[3] We need to teach our children to be discreet. We also need to show them how to be chaste, which means "to be pure or moral, to live morally upright." Teach them to be good;

being good is being nice, kind, and helpful to people when and where you can.

It is also important to show them to be homemakers, though this is another difficult area to train women in nowadays. Too many young women don't want to keep their houses up, but they should be taught to do it. It is a biblical commandment. I taught my girls to clean the house before they got to their teenage years. I taught them to cook and to do all the things I could do around the house. When I got to Stephanie's generation, I found it a little harder training her, but she did learn.

"Teach them to be obedient to their own husbands" (v. 5). Isn't that interesting? You have to teach wives to be obedient to their husbands. Why would God want wives to be obedient to their husbands? Well, mainly because He made the husband the head of the household in a Christian marriage. Being obedient doesn't mean wives should do every dumb thing their husband tells them to do; it just means the wife and her husband are in the marriage together, so she shouldn't do what she wants to do without regard for her husband's feelings or wishes. For example, the wife just can't say, "Well, I'm going shopping, and I'm not telling him anything or asking his permission." I run everything by Fred; I ask his permission. I know he is going to let me go anyway, but I always ask. I don't just take it for granted.

Communicating about these matters is one way he and I look out for each other. Fred can be a bit helpless sometimes. I have to make everything really plain for him. The first time the girls and I took a day off and went shopping, we stayed until the mall closed and then went to get something to eat.

It was almost eleven o'clock at night when I got home, and my poor husband had nothing to eat all day. There was really food for him to fix, but he prefers that I fix all his meals. Now when I go out, I fix something specifically for him that he can eat as-is or that just needs to be heated in the microwave. Fred has also taken to going out to eat or to a movie with Frederick and my sons-in-law when I go out with the girls.

Even when it comes to my giving money away, I always ask my husband's permission. He usually lets me do what I want to do, but still I ask him, because I want to be obedient. Sometimes he suggests another direction he wants me to take. It is best for the wife to be obedient, as the Bible says; it makes the home run more smoothly.

> Likewise exhort the young men to be sober-minded, in all things showing yourself to be a pattern [example] of good works; in doctrine [that is, in teaching] showing integrity, reverence, incorruptibility...
>
> —TITUS 2:6–7

We need to teach our young men to live sound lifestyles, showing integrity. There is such a lack of integrity in this day and age, which is why we have so much corruption all around us. There are many people who call themselves Christians but don't do what the Word of God says. They learn to quote the Bible, but they don't live it. They have a life for church, and then they have a life apart from the church. Fred and I have one life; whatever you see at church is the way we are at home. We are not going to act one way at the church and another way when we are somewhere else. Unfortunately, that is the story of a lot of so-called Christian leaders, and that is very sad.

> …sound speech that cannot be condemned, that one who is an opponent may be ashamed, having nothing evil to say of you.
>
> —TITUS 2:8

After all the years Fred and I have been married, nobody can point a finger and say they ever caught us doing anything wrong. They may lie, which is fine, but as my husband always says, "Let them lie; just don't let it be true." We let people say whatever they want to because we know God is going to back up the truth. We stand strong today in our marriage and in our commitment to the Lord because we made rules for ourselves to do things the right way. We made Jesus the center of our lives, and He is a good example to follow.

Look again at Titus 2:6, where it says, "Likewise, exhort the young men to be sober-minded." That is so very important because if young people today are not taught to be morally right-minded, they won't know what to do when temptation comes. Their decision-making will go down to the level of how they feel, with their hormones running wild. If no one talks to them about the traps Satan sets for young men through sex and drugs and all the other things out there, they are going to go the way of the flesh. The flesh is going to tell them what to do, and they are going to follow it. That is why they need to be in a church where the uncompromising Word of God is being taught and there is a strong youth ministry that is geared to teaching young people about the traps that are set for them. This will help them avoid the mistakes that many before them have fallen into.

There are simply too many casualties in the body of Christ—too many marriages that have gone on the rocks for no reason, disobedient children, teenagers out of control, church members out of control, pastors and church leaders out of control. We hear of stories all the time of pastors falling. Why? Because they will not discipline their flesh. If anyone should be more like Jesus, it should be the pastors and church leaders. Even the volunteers should guard their behavior. We hear far too many stories of our church volunteers who find themselves in trouble because they didn't treat their wife or husband right or because they weren't doing right by their parents. They are not doing what the Word of God says. They don't realize that payday is coming. There is a time when we all will have to give an account of our actions, and I would not want to be in some of these people's shoes when that day comes.

Fred and I have made a great effort not to mistreat each other or other people, and we are at a place now where we can prove that God's Word works because we have operated by its principles. It is an awesome life to live for God.

The Bible tells us to follow the Word and live the good life God wants us to live.

> My son, keep [obey] my words, and treasure my commands within you. Keep my commands and live, And my law as the apple of your eye.
> —Proverbs 7:1–2

Proverbs 7:5 tells the young men why they need to follow verses 1–2:

> That they may keep you from the immoral woman,
> From the seductress who flatters with her words.

Proverbs 7:17–27 tell us how the seductress tricks and traps him.

> "I have perfumed my bed with myrrh, aloes, and cinnamon. Come, let us take our fill of love until morning; Let us delight ourselves with love. For my husband is not at home; He has gone on a long journey; He has taken a bag of money with him, And will come home on the appointed day." With her enticing speech she caused him to yield, With her flattering lips she seduced him. Immediately he went after her, as an ox goes to the slaughter, Or as a fool to the correction of the stocks, Till an arrow struck his liver. As a bird hastens to the snare, He did not know it would cost his life.
>
> —PROVERBS 7:17–23

How many husbands have been stupid, not following what they were supposed to do, and found that it caused them to lose their loved ones, families, and even in some cases their lives?

> Now therefore, listen to me, my children; Pay attention to the words of my mouth: Do not let your heart turn aside to her ways, Do not stray into her paths; For she has cast down many wounded,

And all who were slain by her were strong men.
Her house is the way to hell, Descending to the
chambers of death.

—PROVERBS 17:24–27

These things are still going on today. People are still being fooled. Men are leaving their wives of seventeen years, twenty-five years, thirty-two years, and even thirty-eight years. That is ridiculous. Young Christian men need to avoid this kind of lifestyle. Every time I meet with our young people and the youth of the church I urge them to avoid the world's way of finding excitement. I have seen what can happen to people who do things the way the world does it. Don't go in that direction if you want your life to be blessed.

A lot of times young men wear themselves out before their time because they are going by how they feel, and when they get older they don't have any life left. Fred and I still have a very good intimate life, even at our ages. I never thought it would be like this. I thought it would be over, but it isn't because we didn't desecrate our bodies in any way. Fred does talk about some of the things he did when he was young, but he did all of that experimentation before he was eighteen years old. It sounds like he has been through all kinds of things, but all of the bad stuff he did with women happened before he met me. We got married when I was nineteen, and he has been a good guy since we have been married. That is why he has lasted a long time. We committed our lives to the Lord, and we're still being blessed because of it.

Taking Control of the Flesh

We need to crucify the flesh, the self-centeredness, the arrogance, rebellious ideas, attitudes, and pride. We need to kill all of that. We need to take control of our souls and our bodies. Men, crucify that sexual desire to go after women; crucify that idea of wanting to have an affair outside of the marriage. Men and women need to save themselves for their spouse.

Luke 21:19 says, "By your patience possess your souls." *Possess your souls* means taking control of your soulish area. Your soul is made up of your will; emotions; desires; and your intellect, which includes the affection, mind, reason, and understanding. Your affections should be based on the right motive, and your emotions and desires should be godly. Remember, though your spirit is new, the body is not changed yet and will want to do the same things that it did when you were a sinner. Therefore, you—the recreated spirit man—have to take control.

Your will is involved. You have to will to do what the Word says about any situation in life. If you don't know what the Bible says about a particular subject or dilemma, get in the Word! The answer is in there. When your soul area gets out of line and wants to do the wrong thing, you have to bring it back in line. This act is going to take patience, because your body is not going to want to stop doing the things that make it feel good. The Bible says there is pleasure in sin for a season. Because your soul is not going to want to give up that pleasure, you must be willing to crucify that part of your desire.

Crucifying the Flesh

A lot of times Christians don't have the desire and hunger to do spiritual things. They come to church on Sunday morning and then they don't pick up their Bibles until the next Sunday. These believers are not continuing in the Word. As a result, faith in certain areas of their lives is weak, so they make decisions and evaluate their circumstances based on how they feel. There are many Christians who do things the way the world does. I heard of people in our church who decided to live with their boyfriend or girlfriend; marriage was not even a consideration. That is not the way God says do things, so they end up messed up and can't get God's blessings. We should never want to step outside the will of God. There are just too many evil things that can happen.

Luke 9:23 reads, "Then He [Jesus] said to them all, 'If anyone desires to come after Me, let him deny himself, and take up his cross daily, and follow Me.'" Many Christians don't understand what that means. They think they have to give up everything to follow Jesus Christ. That is not what that means. It doesn't mean to deny yourself the good things in this life, even the material things of life. I believe the Holy Spirit is saying we have to constantly be denying ourselves the things that are against the will of God and crucifying the flesh when in tempts us to act unrighteously. That includes those fleshly things, such as fornication, adultery, envy, jealousy, strife, lying, stealing, and all the other things the flesh is subject to do. Every day we wake up, if we still have some of that kind of stuff inside of us, we need to crucify it. Jesus already gave His life for us on the cross. Now, all we have to do is take what He has done and lay aside all that other stuff that would keep us from moving ahead in God.

You cannot dwell on the desires and feelings—bitterness and negativity are desires, too—that were once a part of your life because if you keep taking pleasure in them you are going to start acting on them. You have to take control and get rid of those thoughts. God is not going to do it for you. I have seen tragedies and terrible things happen to people who held on to that stuff. They would not get rid of the hatred and resentment. Some couples come to church acting happy and smiling for people to see, and then they fuss and argue all the way back home. What a fake life. I have seen couples together for twenty, thirty years with all that hatred built up inside of them. It is up to us to make the decision to do the right thing.

It is up to us to kill those things in our bodies that are against the Word of God. Nail them to the cross daily if necessary until you don't have those feelings anymore. Sometimes women will make a snap judgment call about an attractive woman because she looks nice, and they will say something mean against her. Kill that. Don't say it; don't even think it. You don't have to say those ugly things or think them. You are in control. Don't just hate somebody because of what they look like. God has given you all you need for yourself. He is not a respecter of persons (Rom. 2:11, KJV). He wouldn't bless that person and not bless you where you need to be blessed. You need to train yourself to kill that stuff that is in you. If more people in the body of Christ were doing the Word, how much more would we affect the world around us for God? If we don't kill those ungodly things in our lives, they will just go on and on.

Temperate and Moderate in What We Do

Movie stars, entertainers, and sports figures do a great job of taking care of their bodies, but it's all to receive a corruptible crown. They will exercise, have surgery, and get themselves all done up, but they are just doing it to get accolades from men. If they will do all that to receive a reward that is perishing, why can't we submit our bodies for God? Our bodies are the temples of the Holy Spirit, so why wouldn't we want to exercise, eat right, and look our best for God? If you don't do it, it is not going to be done. We keep eating, get out of shape, and get messed up—and then get upset if somebody says anything about it!

I'm not coming down on anyone, but you need to take responsibility for your own health. When you get older and you are carrying all that weight around, you can't help but end up with arthritis or rheumatism and all the other things too much weight can bring on. We have to learn to crucify the flesh that wants to eat too much of everything: too much candy, too much ice cream, or too much of whatever your thing is. We have to discipline ourselves little by little, because it is a growing thing. Whatever you do, don't give up. If it didn't work the first time you tried to lose weight (or whatever your challenge is), try again. Keep on trying until you reach your goal. Sometimes you are going to just have to say to your flesh, "Stop! I'm dead to that. I don't need that in my life." If you don't need it, you can do without it.

If the movie stars can do it, if the entertainers and sports figures work hard to do their exercises so they can be in good shape, why can't we deny ourselves to receive an incorruptible crown? We need to work just as hard as some non-Christians so we can be our very best for God and represent Jesus Christ the way He should be represented.

I have noticed that when some men reach middle age they go through what is called a midlife crisis. For some reason, they think they have missed out on something in their younger years, so they decide to leave their wives of thirty years or more, thinking that the grass is greener on the other side. They find out much later that they left the person that really cared for them the most. Men, you need to think about what you are doing before you make any move that will destroy your family relationships. You can kill the desire and urge to leave your family. You don't have to act on that desire. Crucify it. Something is very wrong with a person who is willing to throw away ten, seventeen, twenty, or thirty years of their lives to start all over with someone new. Who is to say that you will find anything different? It is far better to try and work things out with God's help than to begin all over again.

Many women read too many romance novels or magazines and watch too many soap operas, which causes their minds to be filled with lust and junk. All of a sudden, their husbands don't seem romantic or sexy enough for them. Then they begin to flirt with some man they think is more exciting. He may not even like women, but he looks good. These women end up leaving their husbands for a fantasy and find out too late that the men they wanted are married or only wanted a short-term relationship. These women usually end up messed up, alone, and wishing they had their husbands back. They have been set up by the devil, who comes to steal, kill, and destroy. (See John 10:10.)

This is what happened to a young lady who was a part of our ministry for a long time. She had the most wonderful husband. He was very good to her, but apparently she was reading too many romance novels. She decided her husband wasn't sexy any longer, and she started looking at somebody else she thought was more appealing. She ended up treating her husband badly and eventually left him. When she found out later she had made a mistake, she wanted her husband back, but it was too late. He had found someone else who really cared for him. If you are going to mistreat your good man, know that somebody else is waiting to take him. You are on a dangerous path when you start to mix up love with lust.

Following After Godliness

We should be so thankful for what Jesus has done to free us from the snares of Satan so that we don't have to live corrupt lives. We can now pursue godliness that leads to a life of joy in Christ, who gave His life so that we could be His own "peculiar people" (1 Pet. 2:9, KJV). That doesn't mean that we look funny. Rather, it means that we have been called out of darkness into His marvelous light to show forth His praises. If your life is not showing forth the praises of God, you are not pleasing to Him. People are running around trying to find out their purpose for some kind of special ministry when they just need to be what they are supposed to be: called out of darkness into His marvelous light in order to show forth His praises. That is a full-time job. Find out what you can do based on your gifts and talents, then use them for good. That is your purpose. Go with that.

> Therefore we also, since we are surrounded by so great a cloud of witnesses, let us lay aside every weight, and the sin which so easily ensnares us, and let us run with endurance the race that is set before us, looking unto Jesus, the author and finisher of our faith, who for the joy that was set before Him endured the cross, despising the shame, and has sat down at the right hand of the throne of God. For consider Him who endured such hostility from sinners against Himself, lest you become weary and discouraged in your souls.
>
> —HEBREWS 12:1–3

No matter how bad your circumstance seemed or seems, you didn't go through what Jesus did. You ought to be thankful for what He did for you and determine that you will be the example Jesus has called you to be to the world. Growing in godliness should be our ultimate goal, and the way to achieve that is to be more like Jesus.

CHAPTER 4

OVERCOMING TEMPTATIONS, TRIALS, AND TESTS

But with the temptation [God] will also make
the way of escape.

—1 CORINTHIANS 10:13

TEMPTATION, TRIALS, AND TESTS ARE constant challenges for mankind. Every sin is preceded by a temptation. The temptation itself is not the sin. Rather, it is what happens after the temptation comes that can cause the sin. The temptation to worry, to have fear, and to doubt God can boil down to sin. When we worry, that means we are not in faith, but faith is what pleases God. We have to learn and to train ourselves how to walk by faith and not by what we see or experience. This is going to take a lot of training and discipline to do. It takes training to believe you receive before you see anything, but if we learn how to operate by this principle of faith, no matter what your temptation, trial, or test is, you will come through okay. Your temptation could be drugs, alcohol, sex, smoking, pornography, overeating, sickness, financial need, or any negative thing that face people every day; but you can overcome anything if you choose to do what God says in His Word.

Temptations first come to our minds, and many Christians think they have to yield to them. "Well, I thought it, so I should just as well do it," they reason. No, this is where discipline comes in—discipline to do the Word over the thought. If we would submit to the instructions of the Bible, we would not find ourselves in these situations. Jesus said in Matthew 26:41, "Watch and pray, lest you enter into temptation." Hebrews 4:15 tells us that Jesus was "in all points tempted as we are, yet without sin." That means, then, that Jesus was tempted to gossip, lie, steal, fornicate, and do all the other negative things that we are tempted to do. Yet He didn't do them or this scripture would not be true. Jesus did not commit sin. He did not yield to the temptation, and that means we don't have to yield to temptation either because Jesus is our example. Keep in mind that Jesus didn't live a sinless life because He is God. He didn't come to earth as God. He came as man, a man subject to the all the negativities of mankind. He chose not to sin or yield to the temptations that presented themselves to Him. This means that since He operated sinless, He knows we can do the same. And we can. It is just a matter of our choice.

James 4:7 tells us, "Submit to God. Resist the devil and he will flee from you." That is how Jesus over came His temptations, trials, and tests. The key is to submit to God. How do we submit to God? We submit by doing the Word. I said earlier that in the Word there is a solution or an answer for every problem we face in life. For instance, the temptation to do drugs and drink alcohol is against the body. Since the Word says your body is the temple of the Holy Spirit, if you want to be free of that, then you have to choose to honor the temple and not put anything in your body that would hurt or destroy it. You have to choose not to do it, just as Jesus chose not to yield to temptation. In fact, apart from Jesus Christ it is difficult to overcome temptation, because when you're a sinner you don't have much control over what you do. Resisting the devil is a full-time job, because he is never going to stop coming at you. If you don't resist him and the thoughts he brings to your mind, those thoughts will eventually end up influencing your body.

I know resisting temptation is easier said than done, but you have to start somewhere. You need to resist the very first time you are tempted to drink alcohol, do drugs, or have illicit sex. I think about people who have been smoking and drinking alcohol most of their lives. In their later years, it takes a toll on them. They end up with all kinds of bodily ailments, such as lung cancer, emphysema, heart problems, and cirrhosis of the liver. If they had only said no the first time someone offered them alcohol, a cigarette, or drugs, they would not have faced those situations. I can think about people in my own family, as well as many other people I know, that spent their younger years smoking and drinking because they could get away with it physically. Now they are either suffering from some illness or have even died because they messed up their lungs and their immune systems.

People take all kinds of chances with their lives by having committing fornication and adultery. I know of a particular case—and this could be multiplied by thousands—regarding this woman I knew really well who got involved with another woman's husband. There was really no excuse, because whether you are into God or not you know that you are not supposed to be messing around with somebody else's spouse. A lot of people have affairs, Christians included, because they think they can get away with it. You can't get away with anything. This woman knew that man was married and had a wonderful family. She knew he had a good life with his wife. They had money coming in, drove nice cars, their business was doing well, and everything going good. The younger woman saw this and set her eyes on that man. She was the type who would go with married men and think nothing of it. She kept on after this guy until she got him to notice her. They began a hot affair, and he ended up leaving his wife. While the affair was going on, this woman would call the wife, curse her out, and say all kinds of mean things to her. She actually got the man to marry her, but the marriage was never a happy one. The child born from their union never had a happy day in his life. In fact, in his later years he got sent to prison. Now the woman, his mother, is calling on the Lord for help.

God can only do so much when we plant the seed of sin in our lives, because those seeds are going to come up, and we will have to pay the price.

Be Careful of the Seeds You Plant

We need to work hard at how we live our lives. That is why Fred and I always tried to live our lives right before our children. If they didn't make it, we never wanted them to be able to point a finger at us and say, "It is your fault my life has gone so wrong." The greatest thing I ever wanted for my children was that they know God for themselves, but children have to know God through somebody. Their mother or father is the first image of God that the children see.

People really take a chance when they have sex with people they are not married to. You really don't know whom you are sleeping with, and you can end up getting some horrible disease, such as AIDS or herpes. I know some people have contracted AIDS through blood transfusions and contaminated needles. God knows when it is not your fault, but if it is your fault, you don't have anything to say except to ask for God's mercy. All some people want is for God to come to their rescue so they can get out of their situations without having to do anything to help themselves. It doesn't work that way. Your heart goes out to them, but you can't make people do right or do what they know they should do to avoid the snares and traps of the devil. There are all kinds of warnings against smoking, drinking, and promiscuous sex; but these warnings don't seem to stop some people because they want to do what they want to do, when they want to do it, without regard for the consequences.

In the Old Testament, people were the same as they are today—wanting to do their own thing. Actually, the Old Testament Scriptures were written for our benefit as examples of what to do and what not to do. God pleaded with the children of Israel over and over again to stop sinning, rebelling, and worshiping false gods; but they just would not obey. For years God sent the Israelites various prophets who told them what was going to happen to them if they didn't stop sinning against God, yet the people just would not listen.

Jeremiah was one of the prophets God sent to Israel. He is called the weeping prophet because he was grieved to the point of tears after God showed him what was going to happen to the people if they didn't turn from their wicked ways. Even though Jeremiah wept over them and tried to intervene on their behalf with God, the Israelites didn't stop sinning. And did they ever suffer! They even went into captivity because they would not obey the Lord. It got so bad for them that parents ended up killing and eating their children. (See Lamentations 4:10.)

Warnings against the coming day of judgment run throughout the Old Testament. God did not want to pronounce judgment on the Israelites, but they kept doing wrong, and so they brought judgment on themselves.

In spite of their persistent disobedience, God continued reaching out to them, just as He does with us today. He reaches out with cords of love, telling us to stop doing wrong things. If we would just submit to Him by doing His Word, He has promised to be right there with us through whatever temptation, trial, or test we go through.

Hosea was another prophet God used to warn the people about their continuing rebellion. He told Hosea to marry a prostitute in order to demonstrate the relationship God had with Israel. God wanted to show that He would be like a husband to Israel, wooing her in order to show the love He had for His chosen people. He also wanted Israel to realize that they were being unfaithful to their First Love, the God of Israel, by choosing to serve false gods. Their behavior was no less than spiritual prostitution. I believe that the Lord placed this book in the Old Testament to show believers today that no matter how bad things get and how many wrong choices we make, we can always come back to Him. Nevertheless, even though God forgives us and continues to love us, there are sometimes consequences. We can be assured that God will welcome us back into relationship with Him, but we may still have to pay the price.

Millions of people in our country are dealing with venereal diseases because of choices they or their partners have made. I have counseled with women whose no-good husbands had an affair and brought a disease back home to them. My heart goes out to these women. If you have a husband who goes out running around and you are going to take him back or stay in the marriage, I would suggest you tell him that he needs to get some STD tests done regularly—and make sure you see those tests results before he comes back—if he intends to continue to have sex with you.

Romans 6:13 says, "And do not present your members [your body parts] as instruments of unrighteousness to sin, but present yourselves to God as being alive from the dead, and your members as instruments of righteousness to God."

A young woman who grew up in the ministry and was a member of our church went and had an affair with a guy who was not, as far as I know, even a Christian. She knew better because she had been taught better, but sometimes we get tired of waiting on God and decide to go out and do our own thing. While she was doing just that, she got pregnant out of wedlock and had to leave her employment with the church. Later, after the baby was born, she found out she had AIDS.

In the meantime, she repented and got involved in the church again. (Here at Crenshaw Christian Center the requirements for employee and volunteer rehire are the same: after a transgression, the person has to sit down from their post for a full year. Once the year is up and they have proven themselves to no longer be in transgression, they can once again be considered for helps ministry or employment.) She had been a good employee before she stepped down from her position and we knew she needed to support her baby, so we rehired her. A short time later, she died of AIDS-related health problems. She left a young child for her family to raise.

We all have felt like getting into trouble one time or another, but going by your feelings and doing your own thing is not worth your life. That is why we tell you that you have to learn to put your feelings under control. It is hard to live right all the time, because the temptations are great and they keep coming. Still, we have to resist the urge to give in. The Holy Spirit will help us. It is up to us to call on Him when we need help, but we have to take the first step by resisting the sin. We have to do what Paul said he did in 1 Corinthians 9:27: "But I discipline my body and bring it into subjection, lest, when I have preached to others, I myself should become disqualified."

Colossians 3:2–5 gives us further instructions on what we are to do when temptations come.

> Set your mind on things above, not on things on the earth. For you died, and your life is hidden with Christ in God. When Christ who is our life appears, then you also will appear with Him in

glory [that is, if you have set your mind on things above]. Therefore put to death your members which are on the earth: fornication, uncleanness, passion, evil desire, and covetousness, which is idolatry.

God, through the apostle Paul, is telling us it is our responsibility to keep away from sin, because in the long run we will be the benefactors.

Romans 6:11 says, "Likewise you also, reckon yourselves to be dead indeed to sin, but alive to God in Christ Jesus our Lord." If you are dead to sin you can't smoke, drink, commit adultery, or fornicate because dead people can't do these things. When temptations come, you don't yield to them because you are dead. You can control your bodily urges and your temper because you are dead, so you don't just do or say anything that comes to your mind. You have to act like you are dead; that is what Romans 6:11 means when it tells us to reckon ourselves dead to sin.

Applying God's Word

Walking in the Spirit is walking according to the Word of God. In other words, it is not just about memorizing scriptures. It's about memorizing the scriptures, then applying the godly principles to your daily life so when the circumstances come against you and your loved ones you will know how to cast that care on your heavenly Father and not allow the flesh to rise up and take over your mind and actions.

For to be carnally minded is death, but to be spiritually minded is life and peace.

—ROMANS 8:6

A life of peace is worth more than all the things you think might bring you happiness. I have said it before, and it is worth saying again: apart from Christ, there is no real joy, peace, or happiness in this world.

And if Christ is in you, the body is dead because of sin, but the Spirit is life because of righteousness. But if the Spirit of Him who raised Jesus from the dead dwells in you, He who raised Christ from the dead will also give life to your mortal bodies through the Spirit who dwells in you. *Therefore, brethren, we are debtors—not to the flesh, to live according to the flesh.* For if you live according to the flesh you will die; but if by the Spirit you put to death the deeds of the body, you will live.

—ROMANS 8:10–13, EMPHASIS ADDED

I like verse 12 (italicized) of that passage. It says to tell your body you don't owe it anything. You don't owe your flesh what it is crying for. If it is calling for you to do something you know you have no business doing, you don't owe it that.

If it is calling for you to overeat, you don't owe it that. I always remind myself of that truth because eating is one of the things I have to fight all the time. You tell your body, "I don't owe you that ice cream. I don't owe you that piece of pie." If you give in, you could be putting on extra pounds that could be shortening your life. I have to deal with weight all the time and watch what I eat so I won't put on weight, especially when we go on vacation. When we get back from vacation, I have usually put on a few pounds, so I punish my body. It never wants to stop eating, which means that if I don't set a limit for myself, I will just keep putting on the extra weight. To bring my body back in line, I tell it, "You are not eating for two or three days until you get that weight off." The last time I went on vacation, I handled the five pounds I had gained in the following way: On the first day back home, I wouldn't eat. I drank some coffee and juice in the middle of the day. Later in the day I ate a peach. That was all I had. (I know some people will say that is bad, but it is okay to go on a fast for a couple of days.)By the next day, I had dropped three pounds. The following day I did the same thing and quickly dropped the other two pounds. Sometimes you have to beat your body up to let it know it is not running you.

It is not good to carry around fifty or sixty extra pounds. It is hard on your body and on your heart. God can't make you lose weight. You will have to do it. You are not going to die if you don't eat for a couple days because most people have enough fat in their bodies to sustain them short-term. It is hard, I know. It is one of the hardest trials and tests you can go through, but you can do it.

We have to do what we are supposed to do if we want to be happy. Jesus came that we might have the abundant life. He came so that we might have an overcoming and victorious life, and yet there still are too many Christians spending time being unhappy because they are not married. I hear wonderful stories all the time of people who get married later in life, but while they are waiting they keep themselves busy serving God. This one couple I am thinking about didn't get married until they were in their forties. They knew they cared for each other for a number of years, but they felt they wanted to wait until the Lord showed them the right time. They went on dates from time to time, but they were busy in the things of the Lord. The man was in ministry, and initially he just wasn't ready to get married. The woman did want to get married, but she did not want to push the guy because she knew the kind of man he was. Instead, she just patiently waited and worked in the church, trusting God. They have a wonderful family now, all because they trusted that God was going to work everything out for them at the right time. That is the way you do it—you keep busy doing the work of the Lord, knowing that He will take care of everything when the time is right.

Sickness and Disease

Temptations, trials, and tests never stop coming. Sometimes you just want to fall down, give up, and say, "I just don't want to fight anymore." I refuse to do that. I have been through a lot between cancer, surgeries, and joint replacements; but I refuse to give into the devil's attacks. If you have ever been attacked with cancer, every time something goes wrong with your body, the devil starts shooting thoughts into your mind a mile a minute that the cancer is coming back. I had to just make a stand and say, "No, it is not, devil. I cast that thought down in the name of Jesus." I realize that some of the physical attacks I experienced later happened to me because I did not take care of the cancer soon enough. As a result, other parts of my body got messed up.

I had to have a hip replacement in 1992. A few years later, the replacement had to be replaced. The doctors said the hipbone was not strong enough to keep the replacement in place, so the replacement metal was breaking away from the bone, which caused me to experience severe pain. I had to submit to the Word, like it says in 2 Corinthians 10:5: "Casting down arguments [or, "imaginations," KJV] and every high thing that exalts itself against the knowledge of God, bringing every thought into captivity to the obedience of Christ." I had to bring my thoughts in line with God's Word. I had to tell myself over and over again—especially when that pain was most severe—what the Bible says in 1 Peter 2:24, that with Jesus' stripes I was healed. No matter what the enemy tried to make me feel or think, I spoke God's Word over the situation. The devil will work on your mind, always trying to get you to think the worse and confess the negative. I finally had to go to the doctor to see what could be done. I had gotten to the place where I could hardly walk. I felt as if my leg were going to break with each step I took. I would still go to church every Sunday, believing I would be okay. I would say to myself, "If I fall, I'm still going to do my job."

The doctor told me that the metal in my hip had just about worn out, and what was left was in a very dangerous place. I needed to have what is called a hip revision. He told me this around March. He wanted to know when I could get the revision done. I looked at our schedule and I told him that I would not be able to set enough time aside for the surgery until December. He said, "Let me tell you something. You could be out of town or even in another country when the hip fails, and if that thing comes completely loose, you will be in a lot of trouble. That metal will send poison all over your body, and it will be very hard to care for that." When the doctor told me that, I could not get to the hospital fast enough. I ended up canceling my speaking engagements to take care of the situation.

That was a trial. I knew when I left that doctor's office what I was going to have to face, because I had been through a hip replacement once before following the damage that had been done to my leg by the cancerous tumor. Believe me, it was no fun. I couldn't move for four weeks. I had to lie flat on my back all that time. I would tell myself, "I can do this, because I know God is with me through it all." The doctor told me that it would take me three months to recuperate. I was actually ready to minister after two months and took my first speaking engagement as soon as the doctors said I could go. If you are in a similar situation, you can't sit around feeling sorry for yourself. If your doctor says you have recovered, it is time to just get up and go, even though you don't feel like moving. You can be assured that the tests and trials never stop coming.

After the second hip surgery, I found a little growth on my neck. Of course, the doctors wanted me to have it checked right away because of my medical history. I went to a specialist to get it looked at. The doctor told me that he could not give me any anesthesia because it would hurt more for me to get the anesthesia than to do the test. I didn't look at the doctor when he came with the needle. I just closed my eyes. Fred was standing right beside me. Later Fred said, "I couldn't believe the length of that needle, and the doctor stuck it right down into your neck. You didn't even flinch." They actually had to do the procedure a second time. I just stayed quiet, thanking Jesus that it would soon be over. When I go through things like that, I think about Jesus on the cross and what He endured for our sake. His courage gives me courage. I never looked at the needle. After the procedure they went and tested the tissue, and, thank God, it wasn't anything. But you still have to go through it to make sure.

I'm telling you these personal stories so that you can see that the trials and tests keep coming to everybody, no matter who you are or how good you try to be. The tests and trials themselves aren't anywhere near as important as how you come out of them. When God is your resource and your source of strength, you will come out better than okay.

Another time I was just walking around and suddenly I felt a sharp pain on the bottom of my foot. Upon examining my foot, I found a small, hard callus. I tried working on it myself to try and keep from making a trip to the doctor over something insignificant. I got some over-the-counter treatment from the drugstore, but it didn't work; it still felt like I was walking on rocks. In fact, I could hardly walk. Again, here came the devil shooting those thoughts again at my head: "It could be a tumor and not a callus." You know how he is always talking to you.

I called my orthopedic doctor, who, thankfully, is used to my busy schedule. He said, "Just come on in and we will see what we can do." I thank God for doctors. In fact, I told my doctor when I went into to see him about my foot, "Thank you, doctor. I know you and God are going to get me through this." When I went in, he took an X-ray to make sure it was not a tumor. After he examined the little knot that was causing all the problems, he determined that it was a type of callus called a *spur*. He just dug it right out and, with a sharp knife, cut it off. I was sitting there looking at him the whole time. While he was doing it I told the devil, "I don't care what test or trial you bring, I will take whatever you send my way. I will stand, no matter what." Yes, it is a stand of faith, but we can do it.

I am not going to tell you that it is easy, because it is not. You are not always going to feel like standing, but that's when we have to remember that as Christians we cannot go by how we feel. Instead, we live by what we believe—the Word of God. After I had surgery to correct my hip problems, my hip and leg required constant exercise in order for me to be able to walk without a limp. There were many days I didn't feel like exercising that hip and leg, and sometimes the joint just seemed to have a mind of its own and would not do what I was trying to make it do. I learned to push myself to do it, even when I didn't feel like it.

In 2004, I began to experience extreme pain in my knee. In fact, since the hip revision, my knee had become extremely sensitive. It had actually twisted and was even causing me some difficulty walking. Once again, the doctors recommended a knee replacement surgery. With the pain I was experiencing, I felt I had little choice. I thought exercising my hip was hard, but there was no comparison to what I felt after my knee surgery. I have heard people say that hip surgery is far easier than knee surgery, and I totally agree. If you have had either, you know that all of it is hard—hip, knee, or any other major procedure like that. I don't give the devil credit for this, because if I had taken care of that tumor when the doctors first told me to, I believe I would not have had to go through the hip and knee surgeries. Even now that some years have passed, my knee still requires exercise. If I know I am going to be standing for any length of time, I will take extra precaution to prevent any severe discomfort. Nonetheless, in spite of discomfort or any other symptoms, I refuse to allow it to stop me. There is just too much to do in ministry. There are too many hurting people who need to hear that God is their answer.

Finances

In the area of lack and want, we know God wants us to prosper financially and materially. In order to be blessed financially, you have to be a giver. The Bible says in Acts 20:35, "It is more blessed to give than to receive." And, of course, it goes without saying that you must be a tither. To receive God's financial best, you have to give God your best, and tithing is God's primary way of blessing His people. However, many times we bring financial problems on ourselves by our undisciplined buying. That was a real problem for Fred and me during our early years of marriage. We could not tithe even though we wanted to; we were in just too much debt. Fred, however, was determined that we would do what we could to please God, and tithing was an important thing for us to do. When we began to tithe, God began to move in our finances. We also concentrated on getting out of debt by not buying anything for the family until our bills got under control. One year, we did not buy any Christmas gifts even for the children, because we didn't want to make any debt. We paid off one bill instead. Eventually we got out of debt, and we have never been in any debt since, nor have we ever stopped tithing.

Sometimes people will stop tithing to pay a bill or to make a special purchase, but this is a definite no-no. Once you start tithing, you don't want to become a God-robber again, because doing so will only open the door for the devil to come in and rob you. Take control of your spending. If you can't afford something, don't buy it. They will not stop making whatever you think you want. Wait until you can afford it before you buy it. They make it so easy nowadays to stay in debt with credit cards and other ways of charging. We learned the hard way that credit cards are a trap that will keep you in debt and destroy your peace of mind. You have to exercise control over your credit cards or you will stay in debt.

Marriage

Another area that will be tested and tried is your marriage. I feel led to share this because there are a lot of young wives who have a problem in submitting to their husbands. First Corinthians 7:1–5 informs us:

> Now concerning the things of which you wrote to me: It is good for a man not to touch a woman. Nevertheless, because of sexual immorality, let each man have his own wife, and let each woman have her own husband. Let the husband render to his wife the affection due her, and likewise also

the wife to her husband. The wife does not have authority over her own body, but the husband does. And likewise the husband does not have authority over his own body, the wife does. Do not deprive one another except with consent for a time, that you may give yourselves to fasting and prayer; and come together again so that Satan does not tempt you because of your lack of self-control.

The sexual part of married life is so very important. I know that some young wives may think, "How am I ever going to go through this for twenty, thirty, forty, or fifty years? How am I ever going to make even five years?" Some husbands, especially in those first years of marriage, seem to want to have sex every day, sometimes even two or three times a day. This can present a challenge for a young wife. Well, this is another area where you are going to have to trust God, because He says for you not to deprive your husband. When the intimate time comes, ask the Lord to help you in that area. In fact, ask Him to help you enjoy this time with your husband, because He is the One who told you to be available for your mate.

This was an area that I had to really work on when Fred and I first got married. I knew nothing at all about sex, and I had to grow into this part of married life. I can tell all young wives it does get better. After we had been married a while and the children came along, I had other challenges. Unlike men, women's problems stay on our minds, particularly when it comes to providing enough food and clothing for the children. If these things are lacking in the home, the woman is not going to be so lovey-dovey when the intimate times come. Her mind is on thoughts like, "Oh, that child needs another pair of shoes; where are we ever going to get the money for them?" With a man it is different. He doesn't care what the problem is at that time. When he feels it is time for sex, that is where his mind is. As time passed, I learned to put aside those thoughts and to enjoy our intimate times. As we grew in the things of the Lord, our finances improved, and as our finances improved, so did our love life. I wanted to do all I could on my part to make the marriage work. If it didn't work, I never wanted it to be said that it was because of me. I found out that this was another area where I could use my faith. I would begin not feeling like being bothered and ended up enjoying the moment because I had used my faith to change my attitude and the situation.

I realize, however, that too much of a thing can be just that—too much. If you are with a spouse who seems to want to have an intimate time two or three times a day, you are really going to have to ask the Lord's help with that. Also, you and your spouse should sit down and talk about the situation and try and come to an agreement. What Fred and I did was to start making dates with one another so that both of our minds and bodies would be free to really enjoy one another. You may even want to get some counseling, either with your pastor or a professional family counselor.

Sometimes women (and men, too) will withhold sex as a way of punishing their spouses for whatever reason. If you are guilty of this, you are going against God's Word, which tells you not to deprive your husband or your wife. Apart from being biblical, this advice is just prudent. When you withhold sex from your mate, you could be opening a door for him to be tempted to look elsewhere. There are a lot of women waiting out there for an unhappy spouse to come along. Some women in the workplace, wearing their cute little miniskirts with almost all their bottoms showing, are just waiting for an unhappy man. If your man is in need, there are women ready to meet that need, and they don't care if he is married or not.

Of course, children are also a real source of trial and testing in marriage. Believe me, parents, you will live and not die. You will get through the raising process. I'm not going to tell you that your blood pressure won't go up a little or your voice won't get hoarse from yelling, but with God's help you will make it through those rough growing years. Like I said before, it would be wonderful if we could freeze our children between the ages of twelve and nineteen and defrost them at about twenty-one years old. Our children did not cause Fred and I too many challenges, because Fred and I had gotten into the Lord early in our marriage. We raised our children in the Lord, so our challenges were not that big or that many. But being in the Lord is the key. Psalm 127:3 tells us, "Children are a heritage from the LORD, The fruit of the womb is a reward." In other words, our children belong to God, and we are actually caretakers of them for Him. Therefore, we have to be careful how we treat God's children.

Ephesians 6:4 says, "And you, fathers, do not provoke your children to wrath, but bring them up in the training and admonition of the Lord." That is the key to raising godly, obedient children—bringing them up in the Word. We have seen this over and over again at Crenshaw Christian Center. Godly children raised by their godly parents in the Word are now raising their children in the Word, and it is a wonderful thing to see.

I know that some parents did not come into the knowledge of the Word until their kids were older. It may be hard to start disciplining your children in the things of God because of the lifestyle the family had before Christ. Sometimes women have had to raise their children alone, after a husband or boyfriend deserted the family. When they suddenly want to change and live their lives for God, it is hard to bring the children in line. Even though it may be hard to do, don't give up on your children. Keep pointing them in the right direction. It may take some extra effort and more time in prayer, but it is well worth your effort to get and keep your children on the right path and stop them from making mistakes that will affect them for the rest of their lives. Children are important to God, and He will not let you down when you are trying to get them on track with Him.

Proverbs 19:18 says, "Chasten your son while there is hope, And do not set your heart on his destruction." This means that, no matter how your children will rebel, continue to teach them, train them, and guide them with the Word, even if it looks like they are not receiving it. Proverbs 22:6 says, "Train up a child in the way he should go, and when he is old he will not depart from it." Believe that, pray that, and receive that.

I know there is a narrow line between trying to raise children right and overdoing it. You have to just let the Holy Spirit guide you. We let our kids be kids. We guided what they watched on TV and the movies they saw. There was certain music that we did not particularly like, but we allowed them to listen to their music because not all secular music is bad. Sometimes when children are not allowed to listen at home, they will when they are out with their friends. We didn't want our kids to sneak around and do things outside the home because they could not do them at home. Children are people, too, and they have feelings about certain things. We encouraged them to express their feelings, but at the same time, they knew they had to follow the rules of the house. The main thing is not to be too hard on your children because if you are you'll push them away from you. Know that they will grow up and put away childish things. (See 1 Corinthians 13:11.)

Know that whatever temptation, trial, or test you are going through, God will help you overcome, that is, if you will submit to Him through His Word. He said in Isaiah 55:10–11:

> For as the rain comes down, and the snow from heaven, And do not return there, But water the earth, And make it bring forth and bud, That it may give seed to the sower And bread to the eater, So shall My word be that goes forth from My mouth; It shall not return to Me void, But it shall accomplish what I please, And it shall prosper in the thing for which I sent it.

We can trust God's Word to do what He sent it to do. Keep confessing that your children are a heritage of the Lord, created to do exploits for Him, and watch God's Word come to pass in your life and the lives of your children.

CHAPTER 5

FULFILLING YOUR PURPOSE AS A CHRISTIAN WOMAN

A woman who fears [reverences] the LORD,
she shall be praised.

—PROVERBS 31:30

I N ORDER FOR US TO fulfill our purpose as Christian women, we first have to find out what our purpose in life really is. I believe the Holy Spirit tells us what that purpose is in 1 Peter 2:9 through the apostle Paul: "But you are a chosen generation, a royal priesthood, a holy nation, His own special people, that you may proclaim the praises of Him who called you out of darkness into His marvelous light."

Our purpose, not only as a Christian woman but simply as a believer, is to proclaim His praises by the way we live. In other words, we are to be an example to the world of what a Christian is supposed to be like. As Christian women, we are supposed to represent the grace and virtue of God.

It is so sad to see the status and position that women have been relegated to today. Not many years ago, women were highly respected and treated not as "the weaker vessel," but rather as vessels to be honored and cherished by society. However, with this modern generation has come a whole new way of thinking and acting. Women now have the freedom, as men always did, to be who and what they want to be, when they want to be it. They no longer have to be just housewives and caregivers for the children; they can also have careers that take them out of the home and help to provide income for the family. This has given women both freedom and income, which they didn't have in years gone by.

Unfortunately, this freedom has not always worked to our advantage. It has come with a high price, particularly with regard to the male-female relationship. Sometimes instead of seeing women as vessels to be cherished and honored, a lot of men see women as competitors—and they treat them as such. Likewise, in their pursuit of this freedom, some women have come to see men, even their husbands, as competitors. They often treat them as such. This competitive spirit is sometimes seen among married couples in ministry. We hear all the time of couples called by God to minister His Word who end up divorced. In too many cases, it is because the wife's ministry work got in the way of the vision God gave the husband. They are no longer submitting to one another in the love of God, but rather trying to outdo one another, as competitors in a race. This is one of the reasons why men and women sometimes misunderstand the biblical meaning of the word *submit*.

The role of godly women is very important to the well-being of society as a whole and as a part of the chosen generation.

In order to fulfill our purpose as a part of the body of Christ, we have to always keep our eyes, minds, and hearts fixed on the truth—that we have been chosen by God to be His own special children. First Peter 2:9 is not just a collection of beautiful-sounding words from Peter. It is a statement of who we are, and we have to start seeing ourselves that way if we want the world to see us as being special. You are a royal priesthood, a holy nation, a peculiar people (1 Pet. 2:9, KJV); are you acting like that? If not, it could be the reason you may not be getting the respect you are due as a daughter of the King of kings. Also, if we really see ourselves as the Lord's chosen people, we will not have a problem with God's way of submitting.

Being a peculiar people doesn't mean that we look strange. It means we are a purchased people—purchased by the blood of the Lord Jesus Christ. Ephesians 1:3–4 says:

> Blessed be the God and Father of our Lord Jesus Christ, who has blessed us with all spiritual blessing in the heavenly places in Christ, just as He chose us in Him before the foundation of the world, that we should be holy and without blame before Him in love.

Notice the Word says we are already blessed in heavenly places. Some people say, "Well, I don't need heavenly blessings. I need earthly blessings." All of our blessings are spiritual or heavenly first before they come into the earthly realm, because they come from God, who is a Spirit. Since God, a Spirit, created this physical world, the spirit world has to be more real than this physical world. We need to realize that we are already blessed, but we have to find out how to make these blessings ours. Ephesians 2:8–10 tells us:

> For by grace you have been saved through faith, and that not of yourselves; it is the gift of God, not of works, lest anyone should boast. For we are His workmanship, created in Christ Jesus for good works, which God prepared beforehand that we should walk in them.

We should be doing good works, which is the way we show Jesus we love Him and, in turn, bless others. Being "created in Christ Jesus for good works" means we are to be doing the same kind of things Jesus did when He walked this earth. Acts 10:38 says, "God anointed Jesus of Nazareth with the Holy Spirit and with power, who went about doing good and healing all who were oppressed by the devil, for God was with Him." We are to be setting the captives free because God is with us, just as He was with Jesus.

Ephesians 4:1 says, "I, therefore, the prisoner of the Lord, beseech you to walk worthy of the calling with which you were called." Sadly, even today there are still too many Christians who are not walking worthy of that calling. That is why we have to keep preaching the same thing over and over until we can get the body of Christ to realize the privilege to which we are called. I covered these scriptures in previous chapters, but I want to talk about them some more, because there is much truth to be learned from them.

But you have not so learned Christ, if indeed you have heard Him and have been taught by Him, as the truth is in Jesus: that you put off, concerning your former conduct, the old man which grows corrupt according to the deceitful lusts, and be renewed in the spirit of your mind, and that you put on the new man which was created according to God, in true righteousness and holiness. Therefore, putting away lying, "Let each one of you speak truth with his neighbor;" for we are members of one another. Be angry, and do not sin": do not let the sun go down on your wrath, nor give place to the devil. Let him who stole steal no longer, but rather let him labor, working with his hands what is good, that he may have something to give him who has need. Let no corrupt word proceed out of your mouth, but what is good for necessary edification, that it may impart grace to the hearers. And do not grieve the Holy Spirit of God, by whom you were sealed for the day of redemption. Let all bitterness, wrath, anger, clamor, and evil speaking be put away from you, with all malice. And be kind to one another, tenderhearted, forgiving one another, even as God in Christ forgave you.

—EPHESIANS 4:20–32

This is how we show forth the praises of Him who has called us out of darkness into His marvelous light: by being obedient to His Word. In verse 22, Paul tells us to put off the "old man," the way we lived before we became born again. It is the part of our nature that is corrupt according to deceitful lusts. Though the Word is being spread throughout the world today by radio, television, books, and recordings, there are just too many believers still operating in the old man. They are not letting the life of Christ be manifested in their lives. They have received Jesus as Savior, but they are lacking when it comes to allowing Him to be Lord over their actions.

Wherever I go to speak, I can't stop talking about the need for Christians to represent Christ better than we do. Most times, you can hardly tell Christians from people in the world because their lifestyles are not that much different. Too many Christians go where the world goes, drink what the world drinks, and do things the way the world does things. Some people have told me that they have heard others say, "I don't want to go and hear Dr. Betty preach. She is just going to say the same thing." Well, I will keep saying the same thing until we all start living the same godly way! We are not going to get total victory in our lives until we decide to put off the old man. As long as I still hear about the evil things that are happening in Christian marriages, among our single people, and in the body of Christ in general, I won't—and can't—stop talking about the same godly truth. It is my sincere desire as a minister of the Lord Jesus Christ that we all come into the knowledge of what He did for us on the cross. What He did is still not real to many believers, because if it were, I believe they would do better.

> Therefore be imitators of God as dear children. And walk in love, as Christ also has loved us and given Himself for us, an offering and a sacrifice to God for a sweet-smelling aroma. But fornication

and all uncleanness or covetousness, let it not even
be named among you, as is fitting for saints.
—EPHESIANS 5:1–3

Many Christians go by how they feel. They commit adultery or fornication because they have certain feelings. They justify the sin by saying, "Well, that is just loving somebody." That is not loving somebody; it's lusting after somebody. Committing fornication couldn't be love, because the Bible says to not even let fornication be named among you. It is natural for a man to desire a woman and a woman to desire a man. However, there is a way to fulfill that desire, and that is in marriage. If you do it God's way, it brings peace and joy. If you do it the world's way, it will bring guilt and unhappiness.

Notice Ephesians 4:22–23 again: "That you put off, concerning your former conduct, the old man which grows corrupt according to the deceitful lusts, and be renewed in the spirit of your mind." The way to do that is by renewing your mind with the Word, studying the Word and acting on the Word until it becomes a part of you. When that happens, you will automatically obey the Word when a situation comes up. When you get to the point that the Word has been firmly planted in your spirit man, it will produce a harvest of right-thinking and right actions, no matter what the situation.

I once read an article in a magazine about a truly tragic incident that had happened to a bunch of black people in a small Southern town many years ago. At that time in the South, there were not many places black people could go to socialize. About five hundred people got together in a barn to hold a dance for the black people in the community. It was the first time this dance had taken place, and the cream of the crop, so to speak, was there. The barn caught fire, and about 209 people lost their lives because there was only one door to exit from. Some churches in that area had been teaching that dancing, drinking, and smoking would stop you from going to heaven. They even went so far as to say those actions would actually send you to hell. The black ministers doing the funerals—not knowing what the Word of God said on the matter—told the people at the services that God had used that fire to punish the people for being at the dance. Then they said that all of the victims of that fire went to hell because they were committing sin by dancing. You can imagine how these people's relatives felt, first having lost their loved ones in this tragic fire and then hearing they were in hell.

Now, drinking and smoking are sins because they are harmful to the body, and some dancing—if it is suggestive and is done to arouse unlawful desires—can be sin. However, none of these things is what sends people to hell. It is the rejection of Jesus Christ as Savior and Lord that sends people to hell. I am using the previous story as an example because it goes to show how many of us are taught things in our Christian life that are not in line with the Bible. No wonder so many Christians perish for a lack of knowledge. (See Hosea 4:6.) That is why it is so important to attend a church that teaches the uncompromising Word.

I'll throw this in here because a lot of people want to know what I think about dancing: to me, there is nothing wrong with dancing, per se, and it can be a good form of exercise. It is mainly the places where people go to dance that are objectionable, such as nightclubs where there is a lot of drinking, smoking, and other things going on. If people are dancing to affect another person in a sexual way, which a lot of people do these days, especially when they are in crowded situations, then that is wrong. But I am not so "holy" to think dancing is a sin.

Personally, I have never been one who liked to dance, so I don't care anything about it. I don't have any rhythm, but I don't see anything wrong with dancing as long as it is done decently and in order. Almost every person I know liked to dance when they were growing up. Our children did, and Fred and I didn't object as long as they were dancing at home or other places we approved of, such as at parties in their friends' homes where there was parental supervision. I believe that if decent people provided decent places for our young people to go to dance, they would not have to be out there going to places in the world where drugs, alcohol, and raunchy music and dancing are likely to be practiced.

The thing that I want to get across to you ladies more than anything is that we have been called out of darkness into His marvelous light to show forth His praises. Wives, mothers, and single women alike have a special commission to be leaders who show our husbands, children, and the world the way to Jesus. If we are not imitators of Him, the world has no way to find out about Him, and without Him, the world is lost.

As you therefore have received Christ Jesus the Lord, so walk in Him, [to *walk* means "to obey" When you are walking in Him, you are walking like Him and doing what He says to do according to His

Word] rooted and built up in Him and established in the faith, as you have been taught, abounding in it with thanksgiving. Beware lest anyone cheat you through philosophy and empty deceit, according to the tradition of men, according to the basic principles of the world, and not according to Christ. For in Him dwells all the fullness of the Godhead bodily; and you are complete in Him, who is the head of all principality and power.

—COLOSSIANS 2:6–10

When we have Jesus, we have the best there is in life. Let's honor Him and teach others who are a part of our lives to honor Him by walking like Him. He was so gracious to give His life for us, so let's honor Him by doing what He says do.

A lot of times people go to churches where the preachers don't teach anything about Jesus or how to live in Him. In fact, some preachers themselves commit adultery and fornication, lie, and steal because they don't really know Jesus. How sad. They know about Him, but they don't know Him or what He accomplished by His death on the cross, such as healing and prosperity in spirit, soul, and body. In fact, it is quite likely that some pastors of churches may not even be saved. There is truth in the saying, "Whatever is in the pulpit is in the pew." If the pastors don't set a standard for their congregations to live up to, the congregation will think it is all right to do anything they feel like doing. We hear stories all the time about pastors getting themselves and their churches all messed up because of some woman or a money situation.

The people in these congregations, too, have to know that something is wrong when they see their pastor is in flagrant sin. Too many times people are willing to overlook a pastor's sin because they like the way he preaches, but I tell you what: God is not overlooking it. Those people are putting themselves in danger of never learning how they are supposed to live as Christians if they overlook his sin. They will still be held responsible for learning about God and how they are supposed to live according to the Scriptures. None of us has an excuse, because there are thousands of Bibles around if you have a desire to serve God. The Bible says that those who hunger and thirst after righteousness will be filled. (See Matthew 5:6.) You will never be satisfied emotionally or physically until you satisfy the spiritual part of your life the right way.

Vain Philosophy and Empty Deceit

Notice Colossians 2:8 says, "Beware lest anyone cheat you through philosophy and empty deceit."

Philosophy means, "A search for a general understanding of values and reality by chiefly speculative rather than observational means."[1] In other words, philosophy is people's opinion about any given situation in life. We have a lot of homegrown philosophy floating around today. If your philosophy or someone else's conflicts with the Word of God, forget it.

For example, I was sitting in the doctor's office and heard some women putting men down and saying how much trouble they were. That was very interesting to me, because although they indicated they didn't think men were worth the time of day, they certainly seemed to believe it was all right to fornicate or commit adultery with them. I heard one of the women say, "I'm teaching my daughter that she doesn't need a man. If she wants a baby, she should just go ahead and get pregnant and bring the baby up by herself, because she doesn't need a man. She [the daughter] has a good job and she could do better without a man around giving her problems." Now, I agree that there are men out there who act like dogs, but don't put every man down thinking that all men are bad. If men have treated those women badly, it is likely they have allowed them to do so.

I remember I was on a ministry trip in Norfolk, Virginia, and a lady came up to speak to Fred and me. She gave me a copy of a poem she had written entitled "Two-Legged Dogs." I don't remember exactly what the poem said, but I could see this woman had been hurt a lot by some man. Like the women in the doctor's office, she had developed a very low outlook on men, which led her to form her own philosophy about them.

These examples demonstrate what Colossians 2:8 is talking about when it cautions us to stay away from "vain philosophy and empty deceit." If those women continue thinking that way about men, it will be very hard for them to develop a good relationship with any man. Their expectations are low, and they'll stay that way unless they do something to change them. One good way of changing this kind of thinking is for them to become involved with a church that is teaching the Word of God. They need to learn about the power of prayer and how a life committed to Jesus can bring a change in their way of living, thinking, and acting.

During my weekly Bible class, I often read books by different sociologists and psychologists. One week I told my class, "The more I read these people's books, the more it seems I know about life more than they do." Many of these individuals go by what they are taught in the universities by professors who do not believe in God. These philosophers and psychologists tell women that there are just not enough men to go around because of wars, homosexuality, and men in prisons. They tell women that the solution is to have a man on the side for sexual purposes, even if they are not the type of man they would want to marry. I don't believe the Christian psychologists and philosophers will tell you the same things as the secular ones, but they leave women with no hope just the same because they still say that you might be one of the women who there is no man for. You can't believe for something if you don't believe it is there. As a Christian woman, you have to decide whose report you are going to believe. Will you trust the psychologists, philosophers, and counselors; or are you going to believe God? Without the Word's guidance, the mind will tell you anything, because it is influenced by Satan.

God's Word says that if you delight yourself in the Lord, He will give you the desires of your heart. (See Psalm 37:4.) He also says that He shall supply all your need. (See Philippians 4:19.) If you want a man, according to God's promises, there is a man for you. If, instead, you go about it the way the world does it and you keep running ahead of the Lord and entangle yourself with just any single or married man, you will reap death—the death of your peace, joy, and fulfillment. Getting involved with the wrong man is just plain dumb, but some Christian women do it even though they know better. When the man gets through messing over them, their self-esteem is down so low they think of themselves as a nobody. If this has happened to you, pick yourself up. Jesus has told you who you are. You may have made a mistake, but that is not the end of the world. Start believing God and start doing it His way. I believe that if you are caring for the things of God, that husband will manifest when it is time. God knows everything, and He knows that not everybody wants to get married or will get married; that is why there are enough men for those who desire a husband.

Some of our women get into bondage because they are not married. When some of our beautiful Christian sisters and brothers keep asking them the same old, dumb question—when are you going to get married?—it keeps them in bondage. Then these same people start putting the blame on the woman, which I think is so mean, saying, "If you are not married, something is wrong with you. Maybe you are a lesbian." I remind these people that whether or not someone else is single is none of their business. If you are single, you have to remember not to let anybody tell you who you are. Keep in mind that you are God's workmanship, and you are complete in Him. Don't allow anybody to put you down. That is man's vain philosophy telling you that you are nobody if you are not married. Remember, neither Jesus nor Paul were married, and the Bible tells us they had full, satisfying lives. Hebrews 1:9 says, "Therefore God, Your God, has anointed You [talking about Jesus] With the oil of gladness more than Your companions." That means Jesus had a joyful and happy countenance. Paul's epistles are a testimony to his confidence and triumphs in Christ, in spite of all his challenges. If you are not married, you are in good company.

Sometimes women decide they are not going to get married. I have even seen where some women have gone out and deliberately got pregnant, saying, "Well, I'm not going to have a husband, so I just as well pick out a man that I would like to be the father of my child." They select some guy because he had money or he was good-looking. That is human philosophy at work. A man is not a father just because he makes you pregnant. A father is a man who is going to be around to raise that child and look after the mother. This is a man who will marry you. Who cares about what a man looks like if he is rotten on the inside? When we don't let the Word be our guide, we will end up all messed up.

I don't believe God told us all the beautiful truths that can be found in His Word just for us to decide not to walk in them. Jesus came to Earth to give us joy and peace. He will keep us in perfect peace if we keep our minds stayed on Him. What is your mind staying on? If you are not walking in the fullness and joy of the Lord, there is a reason. It is not dependent on whether you are married or not. Examine yourself and see where you might be missing it.

The race situation is no different. Black and white people both operate in prejudice, to a certain degree, even though people are the same no matter what the ethnic background. The whites don't want their children to marry blacks, and the blacks don't want their children to marry whites. I know of a white girl who was married to a white man who treated her terribly, but there are also white women who are married to black men who treat them terribly. The same is true of some black women married to black men.

The husband of that white girl I mentioned above came home one evening and told his wife he was leaving her. He really didn't tell her why; he just said he did not want to be married to her any longer, and he packed his clothes and left. They had one child, but he walked out and left anyway. She began to lose a lot of weight, and her family and friends became really worried about her. She would go to work and back home, and the rest of the time she locked herself away, tending to herself and her child only.

Finally a friend begged this woman to come to her wedding. She said her friend told her, "Come for fifteen minutes to see me get married, and then you can leave." She decided to go for a little while, but found herself a little corner to sit in so that she wouldn't have to talk to anybody. She decided to stay for the reception because it felt good to be among people again. While she was sitting quietly in that corner, a black man came and asked her to dance. When she declined because she really didn't want to do anything, the guy started loud-mouthing her and telling her she was a racist and preju-diced. To shut him up, she got up and started dancing with him. It turned out that she and the man ended up being very good friends. Later he introduced her to his best friend, and she ended up marrying this friend, who also was black. This black man has made her an excellent husband, as well as being a good father to her child. Initially her family didn't want to be friends with her new husband, because they thought something was wrong with someone who is a different color than they are. Over time she has proven to them that there is nothing wrong with him, and he has shown himself to be a fine man. She showed her family that black men can make wonderful husbands, too. They have accepted her husband now, and, in fact, they have become very fond of him.

Black, brown, and white people miss out on good husbands because of this color thing. There are many lighter-skinned black people who don't want to marry a particular person because he or she is dark. Their families have taught them not to marry a darker-skinned person, so they get caught up wondering, "What are my children going to look like?" That is so dumb. You want someone who is going to love you, and it should not matter what color he is. When it is all said and done, color is not important. What is important is the content of a man's character, the intent of his heart, and whether or not he knows Jesus.

We pass up a lot of wonderful opportunities by following our own philosophy of life. Singles need to get busy caring for the things of the Lord and let God bring the right person into their lives. Let me give you a word of advice, ladies: don't you be out there picking out a man for yourself without knowing anything about him. You could be picking out Satan's brother, and you will regret your mistake the rest of your life. I believe that if you will get busy for the Lord, God will bring some-body into your life when you least expect it. It is never too late for God, which means no man will ever be too late for you—or vice versa.

I know of a few couples that had this very experience. One lady I know had been married to the same man for a number of years, but he died and left her a widow. She was middle-aged, so she decided that, though she wanted to be married again, she wouldn't spend time looking for anybody at that point in her life. She went on caring for the things of the Lord, and she ended up getting married again at age fifty. I also had a brother who was around the same age as my friend. He had been telling me that he wanted a wife, and with all the beautiful women at our church, I knew I could find somebody for him. I did. I introduced him to one of my friends who would always come to my healing class to help me with whatever I needed. I had watched her for years, and I knew she would be good for my brother. She had had a bad experience when she first came to the church many years ago. She met someone who was not right for her, but when she found out he was not right, she didn't let it stop her. She didn't get down and depressed. Instead, she just told him, "You just go on about your business, and I'm going to continue with the Lord." She just kept right on being faithful, serving the Lord and working in the different departments of the helps ministry. She was the first person that came to my mind when my brother said he wanted to get married. They ended up getting married, and they have been married now for a number of years. They have a very good marriage, and she still helps me in the church. See, she was caring for the things of the Lord and not worrying about getting some man.

I constantly pray that the single women of our church will find perfect mates. I pray this prayer all the time: "Father, I agree with those who are believing You for a mate, for needed finances, or for anything that is consistent with a godly life. Father, reveal to them if there is something they are doing or not doing to hinder the manifestation. Reveal to us as leaders in the church more ways in which we can help our people receive from You. We want our people to be blessed and we know that You are no respecter of persons. What You have done for one, You will do for anyone who will believe Your Word and be a doer of it." You have to make up your mind that you are going to walk in obedience to the Lord. There may be persecutions and trials that you may have to go through, but you have to be willing to pay the price. Who cares about the obstacles, as long as you get the blessings of God? He will not let you down if you persevere.

Facing the Challenges of Life

The Bible says that people inherit the promises of God through faith and patience. (See Hebrews 6:12.) No matter what you are believing God for, you are going to have to learn the virtue of patience. I learned through counseling with people at the church that both singles and married people sometimes have problems with their status in life. While some singles are wishing they could get married, some married people are wishing they were single again. You would think that if the singles would look at the married people, they wouldn't be in such a big hurry to get married. In this life, we all have to put up with something. That is just the way life is—nothing is entirely perfect. Even if you have a good husband, you are still going to have to work with that husband until it gets to the point where you are walking together as one. It takes work to do that.

Sometimes married women have made mistakes because they have not honored their husbands the way they should have. They are looking for a certain thing in marriage. They have been reading too many romance novels, so they think things like, "This man is just not what I want, and I don't love him anymore. He doesn't make me feel this way or that way." Feeling is in the soulish realm. Feeling is in the mind. You don't go by how you feel. Instead, you go by what is right, and that is faith. You can make it if you learn to love by faith. You don't love by sight.

Many Christians spend their time not really enjoying their Christian life. I was talking with one of our single women at the church, and she was telling me about this relationship she had with a male member of the church. She said, "Well, I've been going with this guy for a long time, but he has not made any commitment to me." He had been taking her out a lot, but they had not talked about anything seriously, such as marriage. She said they had gotten pretty intimate. I just asked her, "You're not fornicating, right?" She said, "No, but we're almost to that point." You can really mess up your emotions when you go that far. You could tell that she was totally frustrated, but she didn't really know if she should ask him if he was serious about her or not. Personally, I believe that things should be brought out in the open. It should not take you too long to find out if the person is interested in you enough to talk about marriage. One evening at Bible study, her boyfriend came in and went to sit with somebody else, and she stopped hearing from him all together. Her low self-esteem went all the way to the ground. She came to see me to ask me if I thought she should believe for him to be her husband. I said to her, "I know it hurts, but let him go. Why do you want him if he has treated you that way? Let him show respect for you first. You are worth more than that."

If you don't stand up for yourself, then men will take advantage of you. Men know that a lot of women won't stand up for themselves, which is why so many men do this to women. Those men think, "You want me, so you have to take me however I am and whenever I come." We need to change that. If a guy isn't treating you well, you need to say "forget you" and then go on about your business. Ladies, don't let men mistreat you. Follow Paul's advice in Colossians 3:1–17.

> If then you were raised with Christ, seek those things which are above, where Christ is, sitting at the right hand of God. Set your mind on things above, not on things on the earth. For you died, and your life is hidden with Christ in God.
>
> —COLOSSIANS 3:1–3

As a Christian, you have to count yourself as dead. Romans 6:11 says, "Reckon yourself to be dead." That means you are to act like you are dead. If you are dead, you can't be worrying about any man. If you are dead, you don't need to worry about what you are going to eat. If you are dead, there's no use worrying about your finances. If you are dead, you can't get into trouble. You can't commit adultery and fornication. You can't be envious, jealous, or full of strife. You can't be any of that because you are dead. When you are tempted to do any of those things, you say, "No, I'm dead. That is that old man acting up again, but he is dead."

> When Christ who is our life appears, then you also will appear with Him in glory.
>
> —COLOSSIANS 3:4

Don't you want to be pleasing to Jesus when He appears? He has done so much for you. Don't you want to be pure and right when you have to stand before Him? We can be because verse 5 tells us what to do:

> Therefore put to death your members which are on the earth: fornication, uncleanness, passion, evil desire, and covetousness, which is idolatry.

I like the traditional King James version of this scripture; I believe it gives more explanation of what is being said: "Mortify [kill] therefore your members which are upon the earth; fornication, uncleanness, inordinate affection, evil concupiscence [lust], and covetousness, which is idolatry."

> Because of these things the wrath of God is coming upon the sons of disobedience, in which you yourselves once walked when you lived in them. But now you yourselves are to put off all these: anger, wrath, malice, blasphemy, filthy language out of your mouth. Do not lie to one another, since you have put off the old man with his deeds, and have put on the new man who is renewed in knowledge according to the image of Him who created him, where there is neither Greek nor Jew, circumcised nor uncircumcised, barbarian, Scythian, slave nor free, but Christ is all and in all.
>
> —COLOSSIANS 3:6–11

This is what we want to keep at the center of our lives: that Christ is all and is in all. Verse 12 tells us what to do once we have made Him our focus:

Therefore, as the elect of God, holy and beloved, put on tender mercies, kindness, humility, meekness, longsuffering.

The following verses go on to explain what we ought to do toward our Christian brothers and sisters.

Bearing with one another, and forgiving one another, if anyone has a complaint against another; even as Christ forgave you, so you also must do. But above all these things put on love, which is the bond of perfection. And let the peace of God rule in your hearts, to which also you were called in one body; and be thankful. Let the word of Christ dwell in you richly in all wisdom, teaching and admonishing one another in psalms and hymns and spiritual songs, singing with grace in your hearts to the Lord. And whatever you do in word or deed, do all in the name of the Lord Jesus, giving thanks to God the Father through Him.

—COLOSSIANS 3:13–17

This is the only rule you need: whatever you do, let it be done unto the Lord; and if you can't do it as unto the Lord, then you should not be doing it. Can you commit fornication in the name of the Lord and thank Him for it? Can you lie in the name of the Lord? Can you be jealous in the name of the Lord? Can you be envious in the name of the Lord? Can you gossip in the name of the Lord? Here is your key: if Jesus wouldn't do it, you shouldn't either. This is the way you measure yourself. Otherwise, if you operate in that fleshly stuff, you will reap corruption.

You are going to have to make up your mind to put off those negative things, such as lying, wrath, and anger. Why would you blame God when something negative happens if you haven't been doing your part up to that point? God didn't have anything to do with whatever happened to you. We open the door with our disobedience. The law of God is written and unchanging. When we violate His law, then the negatives will come into our lives.

The Peace of God

God has told us to let His peace reign in our lives. He is not going to do it for us. He has already done everything He is going to do for us. Once we really learn that, we will want to get in line and be obedient to everything that God says, so that we can receive the blessings that He has already provided for us. If we don't obey, then we are going to end up walking an empty Christian life when we should be walking the fulfilled Christian life.

A lot of pastors' wives go through all kinds of challenges because they fail to keep their eyes open. It is true that the pastor belongs to all the people. He is God's gift to the body of Christ. However, it is our responsibility to keep our eyes open to help protect the pastor. There are women who are trying to tempt the pastor. We need to watch out for these kinds of women and make sure they are exposed when they do things like that. Though anointed of God, the pastor is also a man, and he can fall into a trap if he is not careful. Believe me, it happens more often than people think. Watch and pray for your pastor and church leaders so that they will fulfill their assignments from God to the best of their abilities.

We have to treat one another in a godly way. We have to love one another so much that we don't want to put anyone in a position to commit sin. When you cause a brother in Christ to commit fornication or adultery, you are not only sinning against your own body but you are causing him to sin. The Bible tells us that there is a lot of sickness and disease in the body of Christ because people fail to rightly discern the Lord's body; we don't treat our bodies or other members of the body of Christ with discernment and respect. First Corinthians 11:30 says, "For this reason many are weak and sick among you, and many sleep."

Some women are good at tempting men. These women tempt men by the way they dress and by the way they carry themselves. Sadly, they are going to have to answer to God for their actions. I know of a pastor's wife who went through a very traumatic situation in her marriage. She and her husband had been married for more than twenty years, and they had six children together. He had a girlfriend on the side, and they had three children that were the same ages as some of the six children he had by his wife. I don't know how his wife found out about it, but she did. When she talked to him about it, he jumped on her and beat her up.

You can't tell me that God wants you in that type of situation. Of course, that pastor's wife had to file for a divorce, but think of the shame and sadness all of his children will have to go through. You would be amazed at the things that people put up with, and God doesn't want you to go through anything like that. However, God has given us a free will and it is up to us to decide not to live in situations like that. He is not going to come down here and do it for us, but He will give us the strength and courage to do what we have to do to get out of such situations.

Sometimes, these poor women who find themselves in circumstances of unfaithful husbands will say, "Well, I didn't do anything about it because I didn't know what God wanted me to do." God has made it clear through His Word how husbands and wives should treat each other. If you are suffering in a marriage, then God expects you to do something about it. I know of another woman whose husband mistreated her for forty-six years; she just stayed in that relationship and took it all. That is not God's will for you. Ministers and pastors cannot tell people what to do, but we can give you some guidelines. If you are in a situation where it is causing you stress and worry all the time, you need to do something about it. That kind of thing is what brings on sickness. A lot of people get sick when they get older because they have gone through so much worry, fear, and heartache when they were younger.

I used to be a person who worried a lot because I came from a family of worriers. After I found out about the Word of God and how to apply it to my life, I overcame worrying. I read that "God has not given us a spirit of fear, but of power and of love and of a sound mind" (2 Tim. 1:7). I had to believe that, confess it, and act on this truth. Then He told me, "Be anxious for nothing, but in everything by prayer and supplication, with thanksgiving, let your requests be made known to God (Phil. 4:6). That means if you have a husband who is mistreating you, kids on drugs, or anything else negative going on in your life, God does not want you to be anxious about it. Instead, He wants you to take those problems to Him. Through your prayers and supplications, you are giving Him permission to do something about the situation on your behalf. Your requirement is that you do not worry, because you believe God is taking care of the situation for you. You have to have patience. Some people give up because they say God takes too long. No, God can see down the line; we can't. He knows what to do and when to do it. That is where our trust in Him comes in, along with our patience.

Some women have asked me, "How can I not worry? It is all around me." You have to *will* not to worry. You have to decide to give your problems to the Lord. If you have situations where people are sick or on drugs and you don't know what to do, God doesn't want you carrying that burden. You are going to have to give that situation, whatever it is, to the Lord. Why? Because God cares about them even more than you do, and all of your worrying and all of your stress will not help. What helps is for you to pray:

> *Lord, I give You the problem with my husband (or whatever the problem), and I thank You every day that You are taking care of the situation. I believe my husband is a good man who loves me as Christ loves the church; he is not taken in by another woman, and he has completely returned to me and our children. I declare that we are functioning as a Christian family, serving you.*

Then you start acting like what you have prayed for has come to pass, no matter what you see. If you are consistent and will stay with it, the manifestation will come. That is how faith works, and that is why faith is so important. Again, if the situation is too stressful and is causing you too much heartache and pain, you may need to leave the situation and believe God from afar.

If there is anything that is causing you stress or depression, you have to let it go if you want God to take care of it. All of your worrying, struggling, and arguing will not cause the person to change. They have to decide to change, and God will help them through your consistent prayers as you thank Him that what you have prayed for has already taken place. I had relatives who needed to be saved, needed finances, and were involved in alcohol and drugs. I would ask God to send laborers to minister to them where they had need. I would thank Him continuously that I believed their need was met. During my prayer time I would declare, "I cast the care of (I would call them all by name) on You, because you care for them more than I do." When you do that, it releases you to go on and serve God. Then get busy serving God, and those family members who are having problems will be taken care of by the Lord. I will say this, though: if you have not developed a relationship with the Lord, it will be hard initially for you to believe that God is working on your behalf. Establishing a personal relationship with the Lord is the key to faith, but it takes time to grow in faith. You have to stay with it to get the results you want.

A young woman came to see me to ask me if she should leave her husband because her in-laws felt she did not suit him. He was a good husband to her, but his parents constantly talked about her and put her down. I told her that if her husband was good to her, she should forget about the in-laws. She didn't have to go and see them if they tore down her self-esteem. I said, "No, indeed. You don't leave a good man that is good to you. He doesn't put you down. You stay right there with him. He loves you, and that is what matters. He needs to go and visit his family, but you don't need to go if they don't want you to come. You can't stop him from visiting his family if he is close to his family and wants to see them. Remember, they can't do for him what you do. You are the one who takes care of his needs; you are the one who goes to bed with him; you are the one who fixes his food, washes his clothes, and keep his house clean. You can do nice things for the in-laws, like sending them something from time to time, but you never have to see them if you don't want to."

You have to know who you are in Christ, and the Bible says we are His workmanship. You don't have to receive or subject yourself to anything that is uncalled for—whether it is your husband, his family, or even your family. You do not have to believe what they say. There are no ugly Christians. Someone might say, "Oh, you are just saying that." No, there are none, because God didn't create inferior products. There are some people who might not be as physically attractive as some others are, but they are still beautiful because they are beautiful on the inside—in their spirits and in their hearts. Everyone knows of people who are nice to look at, but they are so mean and nasty and selfish on the inside that it makes them ugly. We have to see ourselves from God's perspective. He made us all unique, with our own talents and gifts. We have to learn how to appreciate what He has done in us and to recognize that each one of us as His child is special in His sight. Spend time praying in the Holy Spirit, building yourself up in your most holy faith. Spend time in the Word, and you will grow and learn who you are in Christ and what you have and can do in and through Him. He said that you are a royal priesthood and a holy nation (2 Pet. 2:9). If that is how God sees you, you need to see yourself that way. If you get that into your spirit, no one can say or do anything to make you feel anything less than what God says about you.

Forgetting the Past

In order to fulfill your purpose as a royal priesthood, you have to forget the past. You have to forget anything evil that anybody has ever done to you. You have to forget any trauma in your upbringing and any shortcomings you went through in your childhood. None of that is important when you come into Christ.

The apostle Paul said in Philippians 3:13, "One thing I do, forgetting those things which are behind and reaching forward to those things which are ahead." A lot of people have gone through terrible things in their lives. Women all over the world have been molested or mistreated by boyfriends and husbands to the point where they feel they just cannot forgive the men who hurt them. They have had other bad relationships—on the job, at church, and even so-called friendships—that have left them wounded. We have to move on with God. Some women have said, "How can I forget what this man did to me? I think about it all the time." You are just going to have to forget, forgive, and move on. You can choose to think of it all of your life, but you can also choose to forget it.

The reason I know you can forget it is because God forgets. We are God's children, so we can do the same thing that He does. Now how does God forget, especially since He knows everything? He chooses to forget. In Hebrews 8:12, God speaks through the apostle Paul again to tell us, "For I will be merciful to their unrighteousness, and their sins and their lawless deeds I will remember no more." If you have done something negative in your past, such as committing adultery, fornication, or having an abortion, don't live in guilt the rest of your life. Repent of it and ask God's forgiveness. First John 1:9 says, "If we confess our sins, He is faithful and just to forgive us our sins and to cleanse us from all unrighteousness." Therefore, repent of the sin, turn away from it, and God will forgive you.

Now, you need to be warned that Satan will try to bring whatever you did to your mind again and again so you won't feel forgiven. But you have to know by God's Word that you are forgiven. Some women have had several abortions, and they have carried the guilt of that all their lives. I remember getting a telephone counseling call from a young woman who was just devastated because she had an abortion. She told me, "I know God can't forgive me for that." I told her that God would forgive her for anything she did, if she asked Him to. The only thing He could not forgive her for is rejecting Jesus, because He is our salvation. I don't care how bad anything is—murder (abortion is a type of murder), stealing, lying, whatever—He forgives us. When your past comes into your mind, it is only because of the devil, who keeps reminding us of the wrong things we do. God has forgotten our sins the moment we ask for His forgiveness. We need to learn how to use the Word against the devil, because he is the one that causes us to sin in the first place. He can't make us sin. However, he is the one who brings the temptation to sin to us, just as he is the one who keeps reminding us when we succumb to that temptation. It is up to us to reject it. Satan doesn't want us to receive God's forgiveness. God knows we are not perfect. We make mistakes and bad choices, but God is a forgiving God. He said He would not remember our sins and transgressions. Stop reminding Him of what you did in your past when He has already forgotten it the first time you confessed it and asked for His forgiveness.

We need to learn the things in God's Word that give life. If you just memorize one scripture a week that ministers to you, it is a good start. Say it over and over again until you fully understand it and know it. Also, make an effort to study the Word every day sometime during the morning, day, or evening. The epistles from Romans through Jude are especially good to study because they tell us who we are in Christ. As you read through these epistles and you find scriptures that apply to your situation, underline them and then begin to memorize them. Then when you are faced with temptations, trials, and tests, you will have the Word of God within you to fight the battle. When you have God's Word, it is the same as having the Lord right there with you.

The promise in Proverbs 3:5–6 is an important one to keep in mind.

Trust in the LORD with all your heart, And lean not on your own understanding; In all your ways acknowledge Him, And He shall direct your paths.

Sadly, even though we know these verses, it is evident that we are not acknowledging Him in all our ways. If we did, we would not be on some of these paths we find ourselves following. We have to do what this passage of Scripture says if we want to get the full benefit from His direction. You have to trust God, which brings your will into play. You are going to have to direct your soulish area by the spirit man, which is led by Word of God. You will have to do the right thing instead of doing what comes naturally, which is going by how you feel. You must will to do the right thing, which is following the Word of God.

Sowing and Reaping

If you want friends, you are going to have to be friendly. Whatever you want, you have to sow first. If you want blessings, you have to sow blessings first. This applies to finances as well as to almost everything in life. First there is sowing, and then the reaping.

Some people sit around complaining that our church is just too big to get to know anybody. Here's how to meet people: first you be friendly, and then that seed of friendship will come back to you. There is always someone who needs a friend. Fred and I have been examples of every principle we share with our people. I still vividly remember that when we were struggling really hard in our lives, God sent to us dear friends, many of whom have remained with us until today. They brought some joy into our lives, and they gave our children gifts when at that time we were not able to provide the extra things in life for them. We barely had enough for our own needs. When Fred started out being a pastor, he didn't have many clothes to wear when he stood in the pulpit. In fact, the one good suit he had became so worn in the seat area that when he bent over to pick up something, it tore. One of our members kindly took him to get him a new suit. These are the kind of situations when friends can bring joy to another friend.

We have to apply our faith with the Word. If we don't mix faith with the Word, we are not going to get the full benefits of the Word's promises. We can see and learn this fact from the children of Israel. When God told Moses that He was going to give the children the Promised Land, they probably didn't really understand what that meant. Then God told Joshua to proclaim to the people that He had given them the Promised Land—but they had to go in and possess it. However, there were giants in the land, and the Israelites were afraid. As a result, they didn't go in to seize and possess the land, even though God promised it to them. The same thing is happening to us today; God tells us to lay hold of what He has promised us—financial freedom, peace, joy, love, freedom from sickness and diseases—but many of us say we can't because "there are giants in the land."

People will give more reasons as to why they ought to stay sick, poor, and defeated than they will give for why they should take hold of the victory. They even look in the Bible to find reasons for staying sick, instead of finding out how to get well. These individuals say things like, "Well, Job didn't get healed, and God said Job was perfect." However, God didn't mean *perfect* in the sense of doing everything right, because no human is perfect. Job wasn't sinless, but he had a perfect heart toward God. In Job 3:25, Job says, "For the thing that I greatly feared has come upon me." Fear brought those trials on Job.

The same people that point to Job to justify their sickness use Paul's thorn in the flesh as an excuse, too. They will claim, "Well, Paul didn't get healed, and he wrote over two-thirds of the New Testament. He asked God to remove the thorn from his side, and God didn't do it." However, the thorn in Paul's flesh was not a sickness. It was a messenger from Satan sent to buffet Paul. (See 2 Corinthians 12:7.) In other words, it was an evil spirit harassing Paul. Why people want to believe Paul was sick, I do not know. Then again, if you have not been taught about healing, you can't believe for it. As a result, the body of Christ suffers and goes without the provisions Jesus came to Earth to provide for us.

If we want to fulfill our purpose as Christian women, we are going to have to learn God's Word and then be doers of the Word. We are to exercise the great influence God has given to us to show the world what it truly means to be Christians led of the Word. We can do this by our lifestyles and our commitment to the Lord Jesus Christ.

Our main purpose for being born again and living in this world is to show forth His praises. We are to show Jesus to the world, but we can't do this if we are full of problems. God has provided everything we need to be successful in this life and to fulfill our purpose. I encourage you to get into the Word of God and spend quality time with Him instead of thinking about all the negative things that will draw your attention from Him. If you do this, you will have the abundant blessings of God in your life and you will fulfill the purpose to which He has called you.

CHAPTER 6

HOW TO WALK IN THE BLESSING OF GOD AS A FAMILY

The generation of the upright will be blessed.

—PSALM 112:2

THE CHRISTIAN LIFE IS AN awesome, wonderful experience, but you have to grow up in your Christian walk. Too often, Christians try to grow up too fast spiritually, and they end up believing beyond their faith's ability to produce results. When this happens, some people get discouraged and start complaining, "Oh, that faith stuff doesn't work." They give up before their blessings fully materialize. Jesus tells us in John 14:21–24:

> "He who has My commandments and keeps them, it is he who loves Me. And he who loves Me will be loved by My Father, and I will love him and manifest Myself to him." Judas (not Iscariot) said to Him, "Lord, how is it that You will manifest Yourself to

us, and not to the world?" Jesus answered and said to him, "If anyone loves Me, he will keep My word; and My Father will love him, and We will come to him and make Our home with him. He who does not love Me does not keep My words; and the word which you hear is not Mine but the Father's who sent Me."

When we are doers of the Word, we show Jesus that we love Him. Doing the Word is another way we get to know Him. We receive the promises of God by faith, and by believing and acting on His promises, we say that we honor the Lord as being trustworthy and faithful to His Word.

Ephesians 3:14–20 tell us some important principles about walking with God.

For this reason I bow my knees to the Father of our Lord Jesus Christ, from whom the whole family in heaven and earth is named.

—EPHESIANS 3:14–15

In other words, we are one big family in God.

That He would grant you, according to the riches of His glory, to be strengthened with might through His Spirit in the inner man.

—EPHESIANS 3:16

The way you get to be strong in your spirit is by praying in the Holy Spirit—with tongues—and spending quality time in the Word. God's Word is spirit and it is life, and it is meant to feed your inner man, your spirit. As you feed your spirit and act on His Word, you bring God's blessings from the spirit world into the physical world. It all begins with your love for God and obedience to His Word.

> That Christ may dwell in your hearts through faith; that you, being rooted and grounded in love.
>
> —Ephesians 3:17

Christ will dwell in your heart when you constantly exercise faith in His Word, because faith and the Word are interchangeable. God says that faith comes by hearing and hearing by the Word of God (Rom. 10:17). In other words, you are to be a doer of the Word. You have to find out what the Word of God says about everything that affects your life: marriage, children, finances, your job, peace, joy, or whatever it is you want or need. You must first find the promise in the Bible that fits your need, then you confess it and believe it. Of course, it goes without saying that you must be also living a godly life. If Christ is dwelling in your heart by faith, you will be rooted and grounded in love.

> That you may be able to comprehend with all the saints what is the width and length and depth and height—to know the love of Christ which passes knowledge; that you may be filled with all the fullness of God.
>
> —Ephesians 3:18–19

In other words, there just is no way the human mind can understand the love of Christ, which caused Him to make such a sacrifice for us. But we don't have to understand it, we just have to receive it and appreciate it. We show our appreciation by doing what He tells us to do in His Word.

> Now to Him who is able to do exceedingly abundantly above all that we ask or think, according to the power that works in us.

> —EPHESIANS 3:20

That power is the Holy Spirit and the Word of God. When we make a total commitment to the Lord, He is not only able but *willing* "to do exceedingly abundantly above all that we can ask or think."

Our family has experienced the exceedingly abundant blessings of God as we have increasingly given our lives to the Lord Jesus Christ. The blessings didn't come flowing in overnight. It has been over a period of more than fifty years of serving God. Actually, for myself, I can't remember a time in my life that I did not love the Lord and try to serve Him. Fred, though, did not become born again until our first year of marriage, even though he had joined a church and was baptized. He has often said of his baptism, "I went in a dry devil and came out a wet devil." However, once we found out about the Word and learned to apply it to our lives, it has been a steady upward climb for both of us.

In the beginning while we were learning to grow in the things of God, we had hard times like everybody else, but we stayed with God. We didn't know that much about the Holy Spirit or faith for the first seventeen years of our Christian walk together, so we suffered financially. Even our marriage suffered. As we made the commitment to serve God and became more determined to live for Christ, we learned how to put up with one another. I believe that if we had not had the Lord at the center of our lives, I don't know if we would be together today.

Frederick was a little boy when I discovered Psalm 112. I call it our family chapter. I believe that if a Christian family will follow these passages of Scripture, no matter their challenges, they will come out on top. Our daughter Stephanie was still living at home at the time I began studying Psalm 112, and I made her learn it, too. I knew she would get married one day, and I wanted her to have this wonderful family psalm. When I realized the blessed wording of this psalm, I immediately called Angela and Cheryl, who were both married, and told them to start reading and quoting its verses. I tell my bothers and sisters in the Lord all the time to learn this psalm. My own family lives by these verses, and we have proven that they work.

> Praise the Lord! Blessed is the man who fears the LORD, Who delights greatly in His commandments.
>
> —PSALM 112:1

The word *commandments* is talking about God's Word. You cannot get away from the Word. Sadly, that is what a lot of Christians do. They come to church on Sunday mornings and get what they can, but they don't stay with it Monday through Saturday. The word *delight* means "pleasurable, attractive, delightful, pleasing and desirable." God's Word is to be cherished. How many Christians really cherish God's Word?

How many people find the Word pleasing and desirable? As a Christian, you cannot live without the Word. Where it says "blessed is the man who fears the LORD," it means both men and women. The word *fear* in this context means "reverence." The definition of *reverence* is "to have respect or a reverence for" someone or something, in this case God and His Word. Fred and I absolutely respect and reverence the Lord, and we have taught our children to do the same. However, once children become grown and leave the household, they are responsible to God for themselves.

When you first get married, you really don't know how to be a husband or a wife because marriage is something new for the both of you. That is why you have to be patient with one another as you learn more about each other and grow together. Sometimes it is not easy growing up in marriage; that is why you need Jesus Christ at the center of your life.

Ephesians 5:21 talks about submission. Many times husbands think that submission is only for the wife, but that verse tells husbands and wives to submit to one another. Submission is a two-way street, and it does not mean that the woman is less than the man. Actually, in this verse, *submission* means "to yield." In a marriage, two different people come together with different ideas and different ways to take care of situations. If the two of you don't agree, someone has to yield. Personally, I say there is nothing wrong with yielding as a wife. It doesn't mean you are less than the man; you are just being obedient to the Word. Someone has to yield, or you will run into a brick wall.

Ephesians 5 goes on to say, "Wives, submit to your own husbands, as to the Lord" (v. 22). Maybe you feel you can't trust your husband altogether now, but do what the Bible says anyway. You don't obey God's Word because of the way you feel. You obey His Word because He says to obey it; then you will reap the results. Maybe your husband doesn't understand submission at this point, but God does. He created marriage so that the husband and wife could help one another. Don't spend your time fussing, arguing, fighting, and falling out with each one trying to get your way. If your husband isn't seeing something the way you see it, take it to God. If it is something that will seriously affect the family, tell him what you think, even if he doesn't want to receive what you say. You don't let him or her go on and break his or her head when you know there is a better way of doing something. You don't say, "Oh, just go on and do what you want to do," when you know it is the wrong way to go. However, when it comes to the little things, I believe it is best for the wife to be the submissive one, as the Bible suggests.

To submit effectively on those little things, I learned to just ignore Fred's temper. I had to if I wanted to stay there and do my part. I told God that if the marriage didn't work out, I didn't want it to be my fault. To me, it didn't matter if I had to be the one who did the yielding or submitting, because I wanted peace in the house. Most of the time, I ended up getting my way, and he would be the one yielding. I know that I am not always right, but when I know I am right, I am going to stand for what I believe is right. If I had not stood for what was right years ago regarding attending church, we might not be in the ministry today.

Fred says that I should not have married him. I came from a denominational church and we were not told how to be saved.

I thought that when you joined the church you were saved, but back then I thought everyone that went to church had received Jesus because I didn't know the Word. When we were courting, Fred would come and go to church with my family and me every single Sunday. Then when we got married, he told me he did not want to go to church on Sundays anymore because he was going to play baseball on Sunday mornings. I tried compromising and said, "Well, if you go with me to church on Sunday nights, I'll go with you on Sunday mornings to watch you play baseball." But he didn't want to go to church at all. Even though I didn't know God's Word like I know it now, Jesus was very real to me. I knew I couldn't live without Jesus, so I decided that I didn't care what Fred was going to do; I was going to church. He didn't know any better, but I did. One evening not long after Fred and I had been married, he followed me to a church meeting and got saved. The rest is history. A lot of women mess up when their husbands don't want to go to church. They yield to their husbands and let their husband drag them back out into the world instead of taking a stand for Jesus and doing what they know is right.

After Fred got saved, he was the one who brought us up to the level we are currently at spiritually because he wasn't satisfied with traditional religion. He said, "When I read the Bible, I see more in it than what I am getting at this church. There just has to be more." He began to search for a better understanding of what the Bible and Jesus were all about. I was willing to live and die poor. I was saved and going to heaven, and that was enough for me at that time. Thank God my husband refused to accept salvation as being enough. He knew in his spirit that there was so much more to God.

Even though we loved God and were trying to serve Him as best we could, we were struggling financially all of our early years of marriage. When the children came along, our struggles took on more struggles. There never seemed to be enough to meet the needs of the children. We were able to buy a really small house, but Fred, in his immaturity, kept us in debt through some ridiculous purchases. One day a salesman came to our door selling an intercom system. Fred was so fascinated with the thing that he ended up signing an agreement for one! Sometimes God would have mercy on us and prevented some agreements from going through, and, thank God, the intercom system was one of the things that didn't get approved. I should mention that Fred always wanted to please God, so once he understood about tithing he found a way to get us out of debt. In spite of our financial needs, Fred did not want me to go to work because he wanted me to be home with the kids. As a child, he was left home alone frequently and didn't want his kids to have the same upbringing. There were times that I thought about leaving, but when I would weigh the good against the bad, the good so much outweighed the bad that separation was never a serious consideration.

He is an awesome, awesome husband, and the reason why is mainly because he is a man who fears (or reverences) the Lord and who delights greatly in His commandments.

> His descendants will be mighty on earth; The generation of the upright will be blessed.
>
> —PSALM 112:2

The blessings of God belong to us, as the upright or the righteous, but they do not fall on us like rain. They just don't automatically happen.

For example, we have to train our children to do the Word so that the blessings will come to them. Ephesians 6:1–3 says:

> Children, obey your parents in the Lord, for this is right. "Honor your father and mother," which is the first commandment with promise: "that it may be well with you and you may live long on the earth."

Yes, children have a responsibility to follow the Bible themselves, but parents have a responsibility to teach their children how to honor them because they don't automatically know how to do that. We have to teach them and stay on them about it.

Fred and I did that with our children. We taught them the Word, and they would put the Word right back on us. They would say, "Daddy, read Ephesians 6:4: 'And you, fathers, do not provoke your children to wrath, but bring them up in the training and admonition of the Lord.'" They loved for their father to come home from work, and at dinner or after the meal we would all have an open discussion sitting around the table. We talked to them about everything. We taught them right from wrong, and we talked to them about the things they had to face in the world and what God expected of them. As a result of our talking to them, we really didn't have any problems with our children growing up, except the normal, everyday things that everyone faces in life.

Sometimes parents have to let their children go through some of the childish things kids do. Don't be so overly spiritual that you don't let your children do anything. Some parents have been out in the world doing everything under the sun. Then they come to Jesus and the church and they cut everything out that is fun for their children. They tell their kids, "You can't listen to this kind of music; you can't do this, that, or the other." I don't believe children should listen to satanic music, but some of the secular music that they listen to is not going to hurt them. We did not altogether forbid rap or rock music in the house. It is just a normal stage children go through. Kids have to have some outlets, but when they grow up, they put it away. We would let our children listen to certain kinds of music, because if you don't let them listen to it at home, they will just go somewhere else and listen. I wanted to keep them around so we could see what they were doing. Our kids could play their music, but they knew not to play it all over the house; they could listen to it in their rooms.

When our children were growing up I was always concerned about them being out late at night. It seemed that the kids, particularly Stephanie and Frederick, always wanted to stay out until eleven o'clock at night or midnight. I guess it is a mother thing, but I just could not rest until I knew they were home safe in bed. It didn't seem to bother Fred; in fact, it would bother me so much that he would tell me, "Poor Stephanie and Frederick! Leave them alone and let them grow up."

One night Stephanie had not come home and it was going on two o'clock in the morning. I woke Fred up and said, "It is two o'clock and Stephanie still has not come home." He said,

"Don't you ever wake me up because those kids are out late."
I said, "But suppose she has had an accident or she is in jail or
something else is wrong?" He said, "Well, if she is in jail, she
can just be there all night; I can't do anything about it." With
that, he turned over and went back to sleep. After he got the
Word in him, Fred never worried about the children. He told
me that once he has prayed about a situation, he believes God
is going to do what he has prayed about, and he leaves it with
God. We prayed for our children's safety all the time, so Fred
was comfortable about the situation because he knew God
was looking after Stephanie and the angels were encamped
about her. However, he did speak to her the next morning
and told her she was never to stay out that late again because
it caused me too much concern. She did give us an explanation for being out so late: she and her friends had gone to
get something eat and they got to laughing and talking and
the time just slipped up on them. She apologized and said it
would not happen again.

Cheryl was the first to stay out late. She had gone to a
graduation party at her best friend's house. When it got to
be about one o'clock in the morning, I called Cheryl and said,
"Cheryl, are you crazy? Do you know what time it is?" She
said, "Well, yes, Mom. But the party was kind of dragging,
and there is hardly anybody here. I didn't just want to leave."
I said, "I know why the party is dragging. It is because you
are still there when you ought to be home. If you leave, the
party will pick up." Sure enough, her friends told her that
after she left the party picked up. You have to stay on your
kids. It is the parents' responsibility to keep their kids on the
right track while they are still under their roof. That training

will stick with them when they are grown and raising their own children.

Angela was just the best child. She always tried to please her father. When she was a little girl, her daddy gave her a writing pen and told her not to lose it or loan it to anyone because they might take it. One day, I heard all this crying coming down the street. I went to see who it was. It was Angela. I asked her, "Angie, what in the world is the matter with you?" She said, "I loaned my pen to this girl and she kept it. Daddy told me not to loan my pen, and now daddy is going to be mad at me." She was so afraid that Fred would be angry with her. She never wanted to disappoint her father. She is still the same today.

The only time that we ever had a problem with Angela was when she was fourteen years old. At that time, Fred was pastoring a small church on West Washington Boulevard in Los Angeles. We had services at eleven o'clock in the morning and at seven o'clock in the evening. For some reason, Angela decided that going to church once on Sunday was enough for her, and she declared that she would not be going to the Sunday evening service. Her dad told her, "We go to church as a family, and you will go with us." Oh, she pouted and pouted, but her dad would not change his mind. One evening we had all gotten into the car to go to church, but Angela wasn't there. Fred had to get out of the car and go into the house to get her. She came out wearing some of her old junky clothes that she only wore around the house, and he had to threaten her to make her go and change her clothes. The church was really small, only about eight rows from the front to the back. Angela would sit in the very last row pouting with her lips pursed and looking ugly. Fred just ignored her and kept ministering as he always did—and he got his point across. She may have pouted and looked ugly for a while, but she knew she had to be in church with the rest of the family on Sunday evenings. We didn't care who saw her because we were training her. Because of this training, look where Angela is now—she is running Crenshaw Christian Center, a $49 million corporation. Now she hates to miss any event at the church and is very involved in the work of God for the good of the people. Sometimes you have to make your children do what you know is right for them, no matter how they act. It is all a part of training them, and as parents, we are expected to do just that.

Psalm 112 is one of the first scriptures I started teaching Frederick when he was a little boy. He was about seven years old, and we would go into his room to study them. He was the only child left at home, so we spent a lot of time learning verses together. Sometimes I would forget the verses, but he would remember them and quote them to me. He picked them up quickly, even though he was only about seven years old.

Frederick attended elementary school on the grounds of Crenshaw Christian Center. Sometimes I would pick him up from the playground after school. If he were playing a game or something, I would usually wait and let him finish his game. On one particular day, I had to meet someone at the house, so I was in a rush to get back home. He wasn't ready to leave because he had just started a game. However, I needed to get home, so I told him he had to come. He began to cry because he didn't want to go. He was crying so loud in the car that I had to turn my tape player up really high so I wouldn't hear him.

Finally, when he calmed down, he said, "I don't want you for my mother anymore, and I'm never going to help you with your scriptures again." Of course, he did help me later, and now he doesn't even remember saying that to me. As our children were growing up, we put the Word in all of them. Nevertheless, because they were children they still had to go through some things. For some reason, when they are between the ages of twelve and nineteen, you can't tell them anything. They have their own little personalities, and they usually don't want to tell their parents anything or want to hear what their parents have to tell them. I would have to make Frederick talk to me if he was in the car alone with me, or I would go to his room and make him talk to me there.

When he would come home late, I would go in and ask him all kinds of questions about what he had been doing. In fact, one time I told his father, "Fred, I think you ought to talk to Frederick about being out late. He is probably out there with some little girl, and they're kissing and feeling all over each other. You know how kids are. I know I have given him the Word and explained to him what to do and what not to do, but the flesh is not changed. You need to talk to him." When Fred had an opportunity to talk to Frederick, he said to him, "Your mother said you were out kissing and feeling on some girl. You don't need to be out late with some girl. You are only asking for trouble if that is what you are doing." The next day, Frederick came to me and said, "Mom, why did you tell Dad I was out kissing and feeling on girls? I wasn't doing that." I said, "Well, you won't talk to me, so I have to make up my

own mind as to what you are doing out so late." Finally I saw
how hard I was being on Frederick, and I began to let up. I
just didn't want him to get into any kind of trouble, because I
know boys can get into things so easily. This is why you have
to keep the Word of God before them and your eyes open all
the time. As Proverbs 22:6 says, "Train up a child in the way
he should go, And when he is old he will not depart from it."

Frederick was having an afternoon snack after he came
home from school one day when he noticed that there were
no napkins on the table for him to use, nor were there any in
the napkin holder. Now, Frederick never heard a bad word
in our house, but when he noticed that there weren't any
napkins for him to use, he said a curse word. I was shocked,
but I couldn't act shocked, because when they are young
if you act shocked they will know what they said was bad.
Then they will just start saying it even more. Instead, I said,
as cool as I could, "What did you say, Frederick?" Just as cool
as he wanted to be, he repeated what he had said. I asked
him, "Where did you learn that word?" He said that the kids
at school said it all the time. I said, "Well, Frederick, that is
what is called a bad word, a curse word, and we do not use
that kind of language in this house." From that day until this
present time, I have never heard my son—or any of my children—use that kind of language.

My granddaughter Niki is feisty, much like her mother
Cheryl. One day when she was small she was playing with her
dolls and using that same word I heard Frederick use years
before. Because Cheryl knew how I had handled the situation with Frederick, Cheryl calmly asked her, "Niki, where
did you get that word from? You have never heard that word

in this house." Niki answered that she learned it from the babysitter. Of course, the babysitter denied it, and Cheryl told Niki it was not to be used in their house again. A few days later, Cheryl heard Niki repeat the same word. She told her, "Niki, if I hear you say that word again, you are going to be in trouble, and you will get a spanking." She told her mother that she would not use it again, but it was in Niki's heart. One morning not too long after having told Niki the consequences of her disobedience, Cheryl was taking Niki to school, and they were stopped at a stoplight. Poor little Niki, who was sitting in the back seat behind Cheryl, cursed the stoplight. Her mother reached over the back of her seat and popped her. Niki has never said that word again. We have to train our children, and sometimes we have to apply the rod of correction. The Bible says that if we correct them lovingly they won't die, and it will deliver them from hell.

He who spares his rod hates his son, But he who loves him disciplines him promptly.
—Proverbs 13:24

Chasten your son while there is hope, And do not set your heart on his destruction.
—Proverbs 19:18

Foolishness is bound up in the heart of a child; The rod of correction will drive it far from him.
—Proverbs 22:15

These are the scriptures parents can use to raise their children, but we have to do what the scriptures say to do.

Nowadays, psychologists and sociologist say not to spank children because this can cause some harm to their psyche later in life. That is plain ridiculous. We spanked our children when they needed it—and all of them did—and they turned out wonderful and godly. We know that our government tells our kids that if their parents spank them, they can call 911 and the police or Social Services will come and get them. I say to parents that you better obey God rather than the world. One of the main reasons why the jails are so full today is because our children are not disciplined to respect authority, and this respect for authority starts in the home. If you train your children in line with the Word, even if they take a detour or two, that godly training will bring them back later in life.

Wealth and Riches

> Wealth and riches will be in his house, and his righteousness endures forever.
> —Psalm 112:3

My husband has always taught prosperity for the believer, and he has gotten criticized for it from day one. We never look to the right or to the left, however. Let people say whatever they want; we are going to obey the Word, and we are going to prosper and teach others how to prosper.

When we first got started, we didn't have anything. As we believed God, little by little, He began to bring us out of poverty, out of lack and want, and into the place where we now have no needs. I remember when the congregation gave us a Rolls Royce. There were so many critical people, most of them not even members of our church, saying, "A preacher doesn't need a Rolls Royce." It all started when Fred made the statement during one of his teaching messages about people having to buy a car just about every other year to make sure their vehicle was in top shape mechanically. He said he was going to believe God for a Rolls Royce because it was a car known to last a long time. That was back in 1985. Well, the congregation decided to give him that car for his fifty-third birthday in 1985. We didn't know what the congregation was going to do, but the members wanted him to have it. They kept giving and giving until they had all the money needed to buy the car. After they bought the car, there were some members who would give him money to keep the car full of gas. This happened because Fred is a man who fears the Lord, who delights greatly in His commandments. Don't listen to negative-talking people, because they will rob you of your blessings. These people have no problems with movie stars and other celebrities who have no connection with or commitment to God driving expensive cars. Why would they have a problem with a dedicated, faithful child of God driving one? Isn't that amazing? Fred drove that car for eighteen years.

We have some wonderful spiritual children who have grown up in the ministry and who have been tremendously blessed by God through the teaching of the Word. They wanted to bless Fred, and they said they were tired of seeing him driving the old Rolls Royce. Fred wasn't tired of it; they were. They decided to bless him with a new Rolls Royce. When they took him to get the new Rolls, the man at the dealership said, "Why don't you get a Bentley?" At first, Fred said no, he would rather have another Rolls Royce. Then he took the test drive in the Bentley, and his whole attitude about the car changed. After the test drive, he said, "I have never driven a car like that! That car is something else!" When they told him the car cost $300,000, he said, "No, that is just too much money. I like the car, but I am not willing to pay the price." His spiritual children were just sitting there listening. Fred didn't know that his desire had already been fulfilled, because God said "He would do exceedingly abundantly above all we could ask or think." These precious kids said to each other, "Well, we were going to give Pastor a new Rolls Royce anyway, so we will just up it to a Bentley." To our surprise they came over late one night and presented him with a check to go and get the Bentley the next morning, which happened to be the last day he could place his order for that year. It was supposed to be a surprise for his birthday in January, but he got his birthday present a month earlier in December.

When you serve God, you don't have to scheme and do all kinds of things to bring your desires to pass. All you have to do is to be a person who fears the Lord and delights greatly in His commandments. If you do that, God will take care of you. Let people talk about you and say whatever they want to say. You just stay with the Word, and you will come out successful.

I know that the people who have criticized us in the past don't really know us. Today, we are giving over one million dollars a year to the work of the Lord. We could have bought as many as ten Bentleys on the amount of offerings we have given over the years. We just do the Word of God. God has a way of confirming the Word in your life. That is how the wealth and riches will come, with peace and fulfillment. It goes to show you that you don't have to do crooked stuff or connive and scheme to be financially blessed. God is no respecter of persons, and He will do the same for you. I can't tell our whole story in this book, but if you only knew where we came from, you would just be amazed. It is because we learned how to receive the blessings in the spirit realm first and then transferred them into the natural world by our believing and confessing the Word of God. Truly, it has been through faith and patience that we have inherited the promises of God.

> Unto the upright there arises light in the darkness; He is gracious, and full of compassion, and righteous.
>
> —PSALM 112:4

People say that one of the reasons faith supposedly doesn't work is because "faith teachers" don't believe Christians will have to face anything or have any afflictions. That is not true. The Bible itself says in Psalm 34:19, "Many are the afflictions of the righteous." What we have learned from the Word of God is not to look at the challenges of life. Instead, we look at the last part of Psalm 34:19, which says, "But the LORD delivers him out of them all." In other words, we don't concentrate on the affliction; we focus on the promised deliverance. There is no way the world could ever think that nothing bad ever happens to Christians. All people have to do is look around in order to see that we go through just as much as they do. Sometimes Christians suffer more because we have an enemy who is constantly throwing darts at us, trying to tear us down. In addition, no one is perfect. As we apply the Word, we grow up into perfection, and it is a life-long process. There is darkness out there. That is why we tell our people to get themselves together while they are well and strong. Learn God's Word so that when the enemy tries to put something on you, you will be so fortified with the Word that you can stand and take whatever he wants to throw at you. We have the Word of God to fight with, and with the Word we have the power to withstand any challenge Satan will try to bring on us.

> A good man deals graciously and lends; He will guide his affairs with discretion.
>
> —PSALM 112:5

I don't see how people can be opposed to Christians prospering financially when God's Word says that a good man will lend. If you don't have anything, you surely can't lend to others.

> Surely he will never be shaken; The righteous will be in everlasting remembrance. He will not be afraid of evil tidings; His heart is steadfast, trusting in the LORD. His heart is established; He will not be afraid, Until he sees his desire upon his enemies.
>
> —PSALM 112:6–8

When we are trusting in the Lord, we will not be shaken because we know He will never leave us nor forsake us. We don't have to be afraid of bad news. You shouldn't get all upset looking for the worst. Instead, trust that God is there with you and that He will perfect all things that concern you. That is what it means for your heart to be established (v. 8). When your heart is established, you are confident that everything will work out for your good because your heart has confidence in God's Word. We just cannot get away from the Word. It is our life and our very existence. That is why when Satan came to tempt Jesus, He told him, "Man shall not live by bread alone, but by every word that proceeds from the mouth of God" (Matt. 4:4). Let your enemies talk all they want; they cannot stop your blessings when your heart is right.

> He has dispersed abroad, He has given to the poor;
> His righteousness endures forever; His horn will
> be exalted with honor.
>
> —PSALM 112:9

The Scriptures say that the man who fears the Lord and delights greatly in His commandments will have his horn exalted with honor. In this context, *horn* means "strength" and "a place of prominence and social standing." I have watched this promise being fulfilled in Fred's life. He is well known all over this country and in many parts of the world. I wish you could follow us around and see what God is doing in our lives. It is absolutely awesome. We give all the credit to the Lord and the faithfulness of His Word.

The wicked will see it and be grieved; He will gnash his teeth and melt away; The desire of the wicked shall perish.

—PSALM 112:10

We have seen Psalm 112 happen in our lives. People have talked about our children and us and told lies on the church and us. However, God has vindicated us each time. When people tell us what is being said about us, we make sure, like my husband says, that it is not true. We go on serving God and teaching the Word to set the captives free.

I encourage you to let Psalm 112 be your family chapter. It has brought us from poverty to wealth, from sickness to health, and from a life of hard times and struggles to one of joy and peace. If you are diligent to do what it says, it will do the same for you.

CHAPTER 7

THE TRULY LIBERATED CHRISTIAN

And you shall know the truth, and the truth shall make you free.

—JOHN 8:32

G ALATIANS 5:1 TELLS US TO "stand fast therefore in the liberty by which Christ has made us free, and do not be entangled again with a yoke of bondage." If we really understood how important this scripture is to our lives, we would walk in the glorious life Jesus purchased for us. God sent Jesus to set the captives free so that we could walk in His liberty and wisdom. Being in bondage means something is keeping you from experiencing the blessed life that God meant for you to have on this earth. What "yoke of bondage" do you need to start walking in freedom from?

It is not God's will for us to be in lack or want, sick and diseased, or living in fear and defeat. Even in this day and time, it is still hard for many Christians to grasp this biblical truth. Many believers think like I used to think years ago—that if I were saved, that was all I needed because I was going to go to heaven instead of hell. The Christian life is so much more than that. However, you have to be taught that, receive it, and live it. Otherwise, you will accept and live with that yoke of bondage, which will keep you from fully enjoying your Christian life.

Galatians 5:6 says, "For in Christ Jesus neither circumcision nor uncircumcision avails anything, but faith working through love." "Faith working through love" is the key to living the liberated life. This means you have faith in God's Word and you are acting in love as you live out your Christian life. The more of the Word you apply to your life, the more you will be able to walk in the freedom and love that Christ has provided for us. When the scripture says, "Neither circumcision nor uncircumcision avails anything," it is saying that it is not important whether you are black or white, male or female, tall or short, etc. Instead, what is important is that you are exercising faith working through love. We have to understand that God's Word is not just a bunch of words on a page, but rather it is alive and has power when we speak it and act on it. Too many times, we want to go by what we see and experience, instead of what the Word of God says.

If I had been looking at what I experienced with the cancer and other health problems, I would not be here today. However, I meditated on the healing scriptures I found in the Word and used my faith in God's Word, and the situation got turned around to my benefit. I used this principle for my healing, but it also applies to living a godly life. It applies to having all your needs met, as well as to any marriage or family challenges you may have. You have to believe the Word will work. You surely can't go by how you feel.

Sickness is a good opportunity to prove your faith, because in sickness you feel the pain and go through some other symptoms. If you are walking by how you feel, you might be tempted to say, "I'm not healed." Rather, you have to make that confession of faith and declare, "I believe I receive my healing." See, you don't say, "I am healed," because you may not have the manifestation yet. It is your confession of faith that brings the results, and that confession is, "I believe I receive." If you are going through a financial need and it looks like your financial needs will never be met, don't look at what you have in your purse or bank account. You look at what God's Word says. Then your confession becomes, "I believe I receive that all my financial needs are met." You stay with your confessions until what you are believing for manifests in your life. Of course, it goes without saying that you are tithing and giving offerings, which creates a way by which God can make a way for your needs to be met.

To live the truly liberated life, you have to go all the way with God. You cannot be a half-stepper. Sadly, many Christians try to exercise their faith and walk in love while they live their lives with no real commitment to God or in an outright ungodly way. Some Christian couples are living as if they were married, when they are not. They are committing fornication or adultery, or they are still lying or cheating on their income tax, and things like that. If you are not walking in holiness, then you are not walking in line with the Word of God. That kind of lifestyle will stop the flow of blessings from God. Jesus said in Revelation 3:16, "Because you are lukewarm, and neither cold nor hot, I will vomit you out of My mouth." If you are a lukewarm Christian, this cuts God out of your circumstances, because He is a holy God and He cannot operate in sin.

Galatians 5:13 tells us:

> For you, brethren, have been called to liberty, only do not use liberty as an opportunity for the flesh, but through love serve one another.

Galatians 5:1 says for us to stand fast in the liberty by which Christ has made us free, but here in verse 13 it says we have been called to liberty and that we are to serve one another. If we truly love God, we will surely want to please Him, and nothing is more pleasing to the Lord than when we show love toward one another.

> For all the law is fulfilled in one word, even in this: "You shall love your neighbor as yourself."
>
> —GALATIANS 5:14

Whenever you are in a situation where you are tempted not to love, think about how you would want someone to treat you in that same situation. Jesus tells us in Matthew 7:12, "Therefore, whatever you want men to do to you, do also to them, for this is the Law and the Prophets." In other words, we should treat people however we want to be treated. That is a wonderful scripture. It is the essence of the whole Bible and the message of the prophets who proclaimed the Word of God. Even the world calls this verse of Scripture the Golden Rule—treat others as you want to be treated. If the body of

Christ would only learn to practice this rule, we could be so much farther down the road in serving one another.

> But if you bite and devour one another, beware lest you be consumed by one another!
>
> —GALATIANS 5:15

It is not worth your time to tear someone else down, because when you do that, you pull yourself down as well. To walk as truly liberated Christians, we are going to have to make a real effort to treat everybody the way we want to be treated. I know sometimes people, even Christians, make it really hard to do that sometimes, because some people are just plain negative, disagreeable, and hard to deal with. When we walk in the wisdom of Christ, which is His Word, we can do it. Philippians 4:13 assures us that we really can do all things through Christ who strengthens us.

> I say then: Walk in the Spirit, and you shall not fulfill the lust of the flesh. For the flesh lusts against the Spirit, and the Spirit against the flesh; and these are contrary to one another, so that you do not do the things that you wish.
>
> —GALATIANS 5:16–18

Walking in the Spirit means walking by God's Word. Your born-again spirit wants to do what God's Word says, but that takes training and discipline. I can tell you from experience that when you do the Word, it is well worth the effort.

The traditional teaching on the phrase "walk in the Spirit" in this verse has been that Paul is talking about walking in the Holy Spirit. My husband teaches that it is actually a reference to the human spirit. This is because the same passage says "the flesh lusts against the Spirit" (v. 17). We all know that there is no contest between man and the Holy Spirit. The Holy Spirit has the power, but because we have free wills, He will not make us do what should be done. It is you, out of your own human will, deciding to walk by your spirit and not by your flesh.

> But if you are led by the Spirit, you are not under the law.
>
> —GALATIANS 5:18

The Word of God is what guides our spirits. We must learn to walk by our recreated spirit man, the inner man; and not our flesh, the outer man.

Living the Liberated Life

The key again to living this liberated life is love working by faith and faith working by love. Both have to work together, or we will not truly be able to love the unlovable. You can love everybody by faith, the way God has provided for us to do it. Sometimes, when you see a particular person coming your way, you may think, "Oh, I don't want to be around her today." Then the Holy Spirit prompts you, and you say to yourself, "Yes, I do; I love her in Jesus." Jesus said in John 13:35, "By this all will know that you are My disciples, if you have love for one another." We can show the love we have for one another if we will just remember that Jesus first loved us, even when we were dead in trespasses and sin. (See Romans 5:8.) To make it more clear, He said in John 14:23, "If anyone loves Me, he will keep My word; and My Father will love him, and We will come to him and make Our home with him." John 15:17 emphasizes this command of Jesus even more, so there is no way for us to misunderstand what He means: "These things I command you, that you love one another." When we love God, we are not going to walk in the flesh; we are going to walk in our new recreated spirits. Love is the thing that activates our faith and motivates us to do right.

Jesus also said in John 15:10–12:

> If you keep My commandments, you will abide in My love; just as I have kept My Father's commandments and abide in His love. These things I have spoken to you, that My joy may remain in you, and that your joy may be full. This is My commandment, that you love one another as I have loved you.

If we love one another, we are going to treat one another the way Jesus would treat us. It is as simple as that. If you want to please God, keep His commandment of love. Then you will have God present on the scene, no matter what the situation. In return, God has promised to provide what is best for us.

We need to stop trying to figure things out on our own. This means telling your flesh to be quiet when it whispers, "But God, there are not enough black men [or white men] out there." Well, tell that voice to shut up and go get someone else from another ethnic group! We are all the same in Christ. God doesn't see color; neither should we. Years ago color was a big thing, but now you see everybody with everybody—and that is the way it should be. There is nothing wrong with interracial dating, as long as they are both born again and living the godly lifestyle. Don't limit God by saying there are not enough black men, or there are not enough whatever. You do what God says, and you will have enough of whatever you need. He didn't tell you to figure out how He was going to do it, so you just do what He says if you want the blessings. Then, be patient. Otherwise, you might get yourself into trouble and put yourself that much further behind by being with the wrong person.

I know that there are some women who like pretty clothes, jewelry, and all that goes with them. If they are not able to get these things for themselves because they don't make enough money, they get boyfriends to help them out. Ladies, you don't need that. God will provide your need if you just patiently wait on Him. You have to learn to use the wisdom of Christ, because there is nothing that comes free. There is always a price tag of some sort. We need wisdom to keep us on the right track when the temptation to do wrong comes.

The devil is no respecter of persons either, and he comes to all of us with his baggage when we are at our lowest. He likes to tempt us when it looks like we are not going to be able to make it. He often comes against us at the beginning of our marriage when times can be tough and there is not enough money to do things you want to do. Satan will send somebody your way to tempt you. You have to say, "Get behind me, Satan." You can mess up your life in one split second by yielding to temptation. You can even end up in a worse situation than you had been in.

People try to put me up on a pedestal by assuming I am so this and so that. I don't think I am any of what they say. I know how I got what I have: because of obeying the Word of God. I did not get where I am overnight. I patiently waited. Fred and I did without fancy clothes and a lot of luxury items we wanted. We even did without when my kids were little, which meant that they couldn't have some of the things that I wanted them to have. They had enough to make it, though, because they certainly knew they were loved.

Then Fred and I learned how to believe God and stand on the Word. God's Word brought all the things we wanted and needed to pass in our lives. Some people don't understand this because that is not usually the way people get where they are. People are often either born into their social standing or marry into a prominent family. I observed that when I was growing up. If someone's father was a doctor, lawyer, or a professional, he or she often had it made. Those kids were invited to be in certain clubs or to be a part of a certain clique. If you were poor, however, the kids didn't even look at you. I didn't care back then, and I really don't care now because I don't want to be a part of that kind of snobbish behavior.

When Fred and I were invited to go to Trinidad to minister, the letter of invitation said we would only be speaking to pastors and their wives. Then we received another letter that said the "common people" wanted me to speak to them. I replied, "That's great, because that is who I like to speak to anyway. That is who I am. I am a common person; and

I'll be glad to speak to the common people." I am a common person telling you that the blessings of God are yours. They are outlined in the Bible for you, and if you will hold fast to obeying God, you will come to a point in life where none of your needs will be unmet. It takes staying with it, using the wisdom of Christ, the Word, and walking in love.

There was a time where I could not afford to buy anything for husband, my children, or myself. My husband couldn't buy me things like other husbands bought their wives. Here I was a pastor's wife, with everybody in our church watching me. They watched every move I made and everything that I had on. I hardly had two pair of shoes that were decent enough for church. In fact, I had only one pair of shoes to wear to church for the longest time, and even the front tip of that shoe was coming off. I would be embarrassed, but I still had to go and be there as my husband's helpmate. Actually, I was used to being without because when I was younger and growing up in Mississippi, my family was very, very poor. We didn't have anything, so I didn't get invited to parties because I didn't have a present to bring or anything to wear. Even so, I don't ever remember being jealous of the kids who were invited to the parties, or the person who had the birthday party. I never got any presents when I was coming up and never had a party, but our parents taught us the importance of loving one another, which made all the difference. My two sisters and I never had a cross word to say to one another when we were growing up. We never fussed or had fights, and we were not jealous of one another. I taught my children to be the same way.

Love is the key to being free or liberated in this Christian walk. You don't have to be jealous or envious of anyone. Love is doing. It is the way we act toward each other, whether we are in the church, on the job, or at home. Love is not mushy-mushy or about kissing and hugging, but it is how we treat and act toward one another. I thank God that I don't have any of that jealousy stuff in me. If I did, I would be a mess now from pastoring all the people we have in our church on both coasts. There are so many attractive women in our congregation that I would certainly wear myself out trying to be envious or jealous of somebody. All we have to be is what we are supposed to be, and God will take care of the rest. God is no respecter of persons, and He loves you just as much as He loves the next person or me.

A primary reason some people don't walk in their freedom is because of what other people have done to them. Maybe their husbands put them down. Friends disappointed them. Many times parents have said things that hurt them. Whatever is holding you back, Hebrews 13:5–6 gives the answer for how to deal with it.

> Let your conduct be without covetousness; be content with such things as you have. For He Himself has said, "I will never leave you nor forsake you." So we may boldly say: "The Lord is my helper; I will not fear. What can man do to me?"

If you have the Word of God, you won't care what anybody says about you. You'll just go on with the Lord. You won't let resentment and fear to come in, because God promises that

He will never leave you nor forsake you. If you want to get the blessings of God, you'll need to forget all the bad things of the past and move on into what is going to help you. First Peter 5:7 says, "Casting all your care upon Him, for He cares for you." You literally have to do that. You have to give God your burden, even though you feel like you still have it. If you will give it to Him and do what He says, not looking at the circumstance, God will take that care.

Stereotypes

Unfortunately, black women have been stereotyped. I read a book about black women called *Stolen Women* by Dr. Gail Wyatt, a well-known black author.[1] She talks about how black women's sexuality was negatively affected when they were brought over from Africa against their will. Dr. Wyatt says the effect of that abrupt transition and of the ongoing oppression their ancestors experienced under slavery is still observable. In fact, she says, it is the root of the dysfunctional way many black women operate today, staying in abusive relationships or allowing majority and minority cultures to dictate their perception of their own sexuality.

Additionally, Dr. Wyatt explains that this history is the reason white society has often stereotyped black women as always being ready for sex. She says that black women held as slaves would often pull their dresses up to get relief from the heat of the sun when they were working in the fields. The white bosses interpreted this to mean that the women were ready for sex and often made the black women have sex whenever the masters wanted. Even after the abolition of slavery, many white people continued to hold the misconception that black women are sexually promiscuous and loose in their morals. These individuals say that blacks as a culture condone having sex at a young age and having an unusual interest in sex. Other related stereotypes are that black women always have their first sexual encounter outside of marriage, have a number of sexual partners, and engage frequently in unconventional sexual practices. All of these statements are lies, but they have nonetheless impacted black women's psyche for generations. In this sense, false stereotypes such as those mentioned above have served as societal dictates, changing black women's attitudes about life. The truth, however, is that black women are no different than any other women. God made us all the same.

The things that happened during the time of slavery have caused some blacks and whites to distrust one another, even today. To overcome these obstacles, we need to remember that each of us needs the wisdom of Christ and the Word of God to overcome these negative feelings and resentments that are still with some people today, even some believers. Some years ago, there was an article in the newspaper about a white priest who had gotten a young black girl pregnant at school. Twenty years later she sued the priest and won, and Fred mentioned this case on television in one of his messages. We have a vast audience of all kinds of people, including whites and Catholics. When Fred's message was broadcast, we received a number of letters in response to Fred's message. One viewer said that perhaps if priests were allowed to marry, they would not find themselves in situations like this. Another viewer wrote, "We don't want to listen to you anymore because of what you said about the priest. Anyway, we know that the black girl probably seduced him to do it." At first, I resented that stereotype, which I had never before been presented with. Then I thought, "I am not going to waste my time resenting something that doesn't make any sense. I am just going to forgive the man for saying what he said, because obviously he doesn't know any better. Because I do know better, I am going to do what God's Word says to do: forgive, forget, and walk in love." Nevertheless, trying to put something off on people like that without any basis is not true and it is not right.

Just as the events of our nation's history caused tension between blacks and whites that may still be felt today, there are still some sensitive areas when it comes to darker-skinned blacks and their lighter-skinned brothers and sisters. During slavery, some blacks lived in the plantation mansion, called "the big house," while others worked in the fields. It was usually the lighter-skinned blacks that were given the more privileged position in the house, while the darker-skinned slaves were relegated to tasks outside. Many believed that the black house slaves would have sex with the master of the house in exchange for favors. This perception has been passed down from generation to generation, such that even some women today get ensnared by the affects of this stereotype, feeling that there is often no other recourse in situations of dire need than to give their bodies for favors. This is why knowing the Word is so important to being a truly liberated Christian. When we know that God has promised to supply all our need according to His riches in glory by Christ Jesus (Phil. 4:19), we can stop this type of attitude and break the patterns of thinking that have stereotyped black women for so long.

In the chapter "Redefining Our Image," Dr. Wyatt shares two descriptions that characterize the black woman in slavery. The first portrait is of "the Mammy." She is the Aunt Jemima-type figure who worked in the house and took care of the white family's children. Usually she was someone who had been with the family for a long time and had proved herself trustworthy. She didn't care much about herself and, the slave masters thought, not even about her own people. In reality, these women were just doing what they had to do to survive by resigning themselves to that life, a life in which they could be comfortable and taken care of.

The second image Dr. Wyatt portrays is that of "the She-Devil." These women are basically considered evil. The She-Devil typifies all of the negative characteristics attributed to African-American women before, during, and after slavery. She is immoral, conniving, crafty, manipulative, and seductive. Sadly, this type of woman really existed. Even more sadly, there are still women like this, even in the church. Let me put it like this: they say they are Christians, but they are in the church because Satan put them there. They show up trying to do their thing, making dates with people who are not necessarily their husbands. Some of them are even trying to get the pastor's attention.

We have women like that at Crenshaw Christian Center, but I'm nice to all of them. Fred told me that a woman I knew from the church, someone he had mentioned in a teaching message, came into his office once under the pretense of getting counseling and then offered herself to him. Leaning across his desk, she said to him, "I want you." He said his body replied, "I want you, too," but his spirit said, "No, you don't. It is not worth it." This woman was the type to dress with everything low-cut, tight, and very seductive. I remained nice to her before and after I found out she had approached Fred. I thank God that I don't have to worry about my husband.

Unfortunately, there are women in the church who do that kind of thing, and that is why Fred makes rules for himself. He tells other preachers to make rules for themselves, too. He tells them that they should never go on a home visitation without another pastor, minister, or their spouses with them. There have been times when a pastor called on a member of the congregation for a home visitation, and the woman came to greet him in some type of sexy nightgown. Fred has experienced that, too. People can make up all kinds of lies to hinder a pastor. Now, I know some people who do that honestly haven't learned to put the flesh under. Some women do develop infatuations with their pastors or even someone else in the church. However, people can and should control themselves through the Word of God. For pastors, though, I suggest that you take someone with you on home visitations so that no lie can be told against you.

There was a lady in our church who I really feel sorry for, even to this day. She really needed to deal with her infatuation with my husband. She had been in the church for a very long time, sitting up close for years, and then suddenly we didn't see her for a long time. One day, she came to my Bible study and said to me, "Mrs. Price, the reason I am not coming to church anymore is because I was just so lustful for Pastor Price. I just couldn't stand it, so I finally stopped coming to church. I never did have anything against you. I love you." I really wanted to help her, but then she disappeared again. It is normal to see somebody who is nice-looking or attractive and admire them, but that is when you have to take control of your feelings. Many times when these women are attracted to preachers, it is because they fall in love with their spirits, or what we call "the anointing." They don't even realize that their spirits are drawn to the anointing that is on the pastor's ministry as gift to the body of Christ. A lot of pastors have messed up their ministries by succumbing to some woman running after them, thinking she is in love with the pastor. When the pastor yields to the temptation, they are both out in the street. That is why we have to make rules for ourselves.

Black women do not have to receive the stereotyped images that society has placed on us, because we have the Word of God to tell us who we are. We can overcome these negative influences in black society by teaching our children in the home who they are in Christ. That is what I taught my children. We talked about everything. Fred and I raised them up without them getting into trouble because we were frank about what was happening out there in the world.

When Frederick was growing up, there were a lot of girls calling the house. I don't know what these girls were thinking of. Parents, we need to train our daughters better than that. I told Frederick, just like I told our girls, "Don't get yourself sexually involved with anyone before you get married because you will just mess yourself up." There are all kinds of ways to mess up, apart from diseases. That is what we need to tell our children. You don't need to bring somebody else into your married life. When you have been out there sexually active and then get married, you'll want to put the things you were doing out there with Sally or Suzie into your relationship with your wife. Doing this will cause distrust and confusion in the relationship.

Dr. Wyatt said that when it comes down to it, all races have the same type of sexual attitudes going on. Whatever background you come from, don't let anybody put you down, saying you are a certain way or a certain type of person. We have to realize that we are all free to walk in the spirit and not be slaves to the flesh. Jesus Christ has made us free, but it is up to us to train and discipline ourselves to walk in that freedom.

Romans 14:17 says, "For the kingdom of God is not eating and drinking, but righteousness and peace and joy in the Holy Spirit." The term "eating and drinking" is talking about the flesh. When it says "peace and joy," it is referring to our spirit man. We can be truly liberated Christians when we learn to walk in the spirit and not in the flesh.

Colossians 3:12–17 is a road map showing the way to God's peace and joy in the Holy Spirit.

> Therefore, as the elect of God, holy and beloved, put on tender mercies, kindness, humility, meek-ness, longsuffering; bearing with one another, and forgiving one another, if anyone has a complaint against another; even as Christ forgave you, so you also must do. But above all these things put on love, which is the bond of perfection [or maturity]. And let the peace of God rule in your hearts, to which also you were called in one body; and be thankful.

Let the word of Christ dwell in you richly in all wisdom, teaching and admonishing one another in psalms and hymns and spiritual songs, singing with grace in your hearts to the Lord. And whatever you do in word or deed, do all in the name of the Lord Jesus, giving thanks to God the Father through Him.

I trust this book has been a blessing to you and will help you to grow and develop your spiritual life. My desire is that we walk and live in the liberty in which Christ has made us free as we enjoy the rich blessings of God from generation to generation.

CONFESSIONS
FOR SUCCESS

FATHER, I THANK YOU THAT:

- ♪ I walk in the liberty in which Christ has made me free, and the fruit of the Spirit—love, joy, peace, longsuffering, gentleness, kindness, faithfulness, and self-control—are operating in my life. (See 2 Corinthians 3:17; Galatians 5:22–23.)

- ♪ I am the righteousness of God in Christ Jesus, and I live by faith. (See 2 Corinthians 5:21; Romans 1:17.)

- ♪ The Spirit that raised Jesus from the dead dwells in me, and I am made alive in my mortal body by that same Spirit. (See Romans 8:11.)

- ♪ Jesus bore my sins in His own body on the tree, that I, being dead to sins, should live unto righteousness. (See 1 Peter 2:24.)

- ♪ Jesus—by whose stripes I was healed—took my infirmities and bore my sickness. (See Matthew 8:17; 1 Peter 2:24.)

- ♪ Christ has redeemed me from the curse of the law, being made a curse for me; for it is written, "Cursed is every one who hangs on a tree." (See Galatians 3:13.)

ⓢ I overcome sickness and disease by the blood of the Lamb and the word of my testimony.

ⓢ The joy of the Lord remains in me, and I rejoice in the Lord always. (See John 15:11; Philippians 4:4.)

ⓢ The trying of my faith works patience. I let patience have its perfect work in me so that I may continue to mature and be strong in faith. (See James 1:2–4.)

ⓢ My heart is not troubled, because Jesus has overcome the world on my behalf and, being justified by faith, I have peace with God. (See John 14:27; John 16:33; and Romans 5:1.)

ⓢ I have not been given a spirit of fear, but of power, love, and of a sound mind. (See 2 Timothy 1:7.)

ⓢ Neither death nor life; nor angels nor principalities nor powers; nor things present nor things to come; nor height nor depth; nor any other created thing will separate me from the love of God, which is in Christ Jesus my Lord. (See Romans 8:38–39.)

ⓢ The love of God has been poured out in my heart by the Holy Spirit who has been given to me. (See Romans 5:5.)

ⓢ I do not cast away my confidence in God's Word. I am doing the will of God, and I will receive His promises. (See Hebrews 10:35–36.)

ⓢ All things work together for my good, for the eyes of the Lord are on the righteous and His ears are open to my prayers. (See Romans 8:28; 1 Peter 3:12.)

ⓢ I have been delivered from the power of darkness, and I have been translated into the kingdom of

Jesus Christ. Satan has no dominion over me. (See Colossians 1:13.)

ჳ   I am a new creation; old things are passed away, and I reign in life by the One, Jesus Christ. (See 2 Corinthians 5:17; Romans 5:17.)

ჳ   There is no condemnation to me because I walk not after the flesh, but according to my renewed spirit; for the law of the Spirit of life in Christ Jesus has made me free from the law of sin and death. (See Romans 8:1–2.)

ჳ   I fight the good fight of faith. I profess a good confession before many witnesses, and I am a partaker of the inheritance of the saints in the light. (See 1 Timothy 6:12; Colossians 1:12.)

ჳ   I forget those things which are behind, and I reach forward to those things which are ahead. I press toward the goal for the prize of the high calling of God in Christ Jesus. (See Philippians 3:13–14.)

ჳ   I am more than a conqueror through Him that loves me, and since God is for me, who can be successful against me? (See Romans 8:37.)

ჳ   I do not waver at the promises of God through unbelief, but I am strong in faith knowing that greater is He who is in me than Satan, who is in the world. (See Romans 4:20; 1 John 4:4.)

ჳ   I let no corrupt communication come out of my mouth. I put away all bitterness, wrath, anger, and evil speaking. I do not grieve the Holy Spirit. (See Ephesians 4:29–31.)

ჳ   I present my body a living sacrifice, holy and acceptable to God. I am not conformed to this world, but

I am renewed in my mind daily with God's Word so that I may prove what is the good, acceptable, and perfect will of God for my life. (See Romans 12:1–2.)

🕉 I can do all things through Christ, who strengthens me. (See Philippians 4:13.)

🕉 I am walking worthy of the Lord in every area of life. I am fruitful in every good work, and I am increasing in the knowledge of God daily. (See Colossians 1:10.)

🕉 I am not anxious about anything, but in everything, by prayer and supplication with thanksgiving, I let my requests be made known to God. And the peace of God, which surpasses all understanding, keeps my heart and mind at peace through Christ Jesus. (See Philippians 4:6–7.)

Notes

Chapter 1

The High Calling of God

1. *The Spirit-Filled Life Bible*, ed. Jack Hayford (Nashville, TN: Thomas Nelson, Inc., 1991), 1727.

2. Ibid.

Chapter 2

The Call to Serve

1. Merrill F. Unger and William White, Jr., eds., *Vine's Expository Dictionary of Biblical Words*, Vol. 3 (Grand Rapids, MI: Fleming H. Revell, 1981), s.v. "serve."

Chapter 3

Growing in Godliness

1. Webster's New World College Dictionary (Springfield, MA: Webster, 2004), s.v. "sober."

2. Merriam-Webster's Collegiate Dictionary, 10th ed. (Springfield, MA: Merriam-Webster, 1999), s.v. "slander."

3. Ibid., s.v. "discreet."

Chapter 5

Fulfilling Your Purpose as a Christian Woman

1. Ibid., s.v. "philosophy."

Chapter 7

The Truly Liberated Christian

1. Dr. Gail Wyatt, *Stolen Women* (Indianapolis, IN: John Wiley & Sons, Inc., 1998).

ABOUT THE AUTHOR

D R. BETTY R. PRICE IS the wife of Dr. Frederick K. C. Price, founder and pastor of Crenshaw Christian Center East in Manhattan, New York, and Crenshaw Christian Center West, home of the ten thousand-seat FaithDome and Ever Increasing Faith Ministries, located in Los Angeles, California. As First Lady, Dr. Betty is an integral part of her husband's ministry and travels extensively with him ministering and teaching the uncompromising Word of God.

Dr. Betty plays a pivotal role at Crenshaw Christian Center. Her love and concern for others have led to the establishment of numerous programs and groups at the church, including:

- Women's Fellowship, which has become a model for many women's auxiliaries at other churches;

- Women Who Care is designed for godly women to share their expertise, experiences, and testimonies to inform, inspire, and encourage other women in the things of God;

- Big Sisters/Little Sisters Program, spearheaded by godly young ladies who are positive role models for other young ladies in the body of Christ;

- Twenty-four-hour intercessory prayer network for members, visitors, and friends;

୬ Alcohol/drug abuse and co-dependency programs provide a means of helping those afflicted with the scourge of drug abuse;

୬ Community Outreach Program distributes food, clothing, and toys to the indigent in the communities surrounding the church;

୬ Encouragement and Cancer Support Group meets weekly using the Word of God to assure participants that they have the victory over cancer;

୬ Vermont Village Community Development Corporation, an organization established for the purpose of improving and beautifying the Vermont corridor in south-central Los Angeles and bringing viable businesses back into the community.

The Prices have been married over fifty years, and they have spent all but one of those years in ministry together. They have four living children: Angela Marie Evans, Cheryl Ann Price, Stephanie Pauline Buchanan, and Frederick Kenneth Price. All of the Price children and their sons-in-law, A. Michael Evans Jr. and Danon Buchanan, work in the ministry. They also have one daughter-in-law, Angel Brown Price. The Prices have one deceased son who was struck and killed by a car when he was only eight years of age.

A minister of the gospel and a popular guest speaker, Dr. Betty received an honorary doctorate degree in June 1993 from the Southern California School of Ministry, located in Inglewood, California, and was ordained to the ministry in January 1994.

For more information, to receive a catalog, or to be placed on the Ever Increasing Faith Ministries mailing list please contact:

Crenshaw Christian Center
PO Box 90000
Los Angeles, CA 90009
(800) 927–3436

Check your local TV or Webcast listing for Ever Increasing Faith Ministries or visit our Web site, **www.faithdome.org**.

MORE BOOKS BY DR. BETTY R. PRICE

Wisdom From Above, Volume 1

How to Live the Prosperous Life and Have Good Success

Says Dr. Betty, "This book has been written with the aim to help believers, especially women, know their rights in Christ, to encourage them to reach for the highest call of God, and to live the victorious, overcoming life."

10-digit ISBN: 1-59979-241-9
13-digit ISBN: 978-1-59979-241-5

Through the Fire & Through the Water

My Triumph Over Cancer

In 1990, Dr. Betty laid in her hospital bed under a possible sentence of death when she heard words of life in her spirit: "This illness is not unto death, but that the Son of God may be glorified through it." Dr. Betty and the Price family share the story of her battle.

10-digit ISBN: 1-883798-33-7 *(English)*
13-digit ISBN: 978-1-883798-33-8

(Also available in Spanish and audiobook)

Lifestyles of the Rich & Faithful

In this book Dr. Betty candidly explores the challenges faced by many Christians today in handling perplexing problems that are hindering them from receiving the promised blessings of God.

10-digit ISBN: 1-883798-40-X
13-digit ISBN: 978-1-883798-40-6

Standing by God's Man

It definitely takes a lot of grace—God's grace—not only to be a Christian wife, but also to be a preacher's wife. This book offers Dr. Betty's testimony of her early years and is a recipe to supporting and living with a great man of God.

10-digit ISBN: 1-883798-49-3 *(Mini-book)*
13-digit ISBN: 978-1-883798-49-9

These teachings are also available on CD and cassette. For the latest information on other books, visual, and audio products please contact us at:

(800) 927-3436

www.faithdome.org

MOST RECENT AUDIO RELEASES BY DR. BETTY R. PRICE

Six Ways to Transform Your Life

The life of the believer should be one of constant growth, marked by goodness, righteousness, and truth. These teachings will help the believer to mature in God's Word and live a life that is far greater than mere existence.

BPD 18 (6-CD)

Wisdom From Above

These six teachings by Dr. Betty specifically speak to the issues that plague so many Christian women and describe how to overcome these difficulties through God's Word. This wealth of wisdom includes such teachings as "What's On Your Mind?" "Making Wise Choices," "How to Deal With Your Issues," and much more.

BPD 8 (6-CD)

Healing Is Our Covenant Right

Is it God's will for Christians to suffer in sickness and disease? Your church may say it is, but what does God's Word say about this matter? Learn the truth about your covenant right to healing and divine health, and then live well!

BPT 1 (4-CD)

A Lifestyle of Excellence

Having God's best is a process of operating in faith and walking in a godly lifestyle. If you want to know what is keeping you from receiving God's blessings, you need this series to give you the tools to walk in God's prosperity in spirit, soul, and body.

BPT 3 (4-CD)

For the latest information on other books, visual, and audio products please contact us at:

(800) 927-3436

www.faithdome.org

F AITH ONE PUBLISHING IS THE publishing arm of Crenshaw Christian Center in Los Angeles, California and publisher of *Ever Increasing Faith Magazine.*

Subscribe or Renew your FREE Magazine Subscription

Website: www.faithdome.org
Call us: (800) 927-3436

This quarterly magazine brings the latest and greatest teachings of Drs. Fred and Betty Price absolutely free to those living in the continental United States. Teachings are geared for the Christian today and cover such areas as:

- ✤ Parenting
- ✤ Health & Healing
- ✤ From the Headlines
- ✤ Testimonies
- ✤ Missions

Keep informed and growing in the things of God by receiving your free copy of this magazine designed to empower you with the Word of Faith.

The Power of Faith to Transform Your Life!